LET ME TAKE YOU DOWN

Let Me Take You Down

PENNY LANE AND STRAWBERRY FIELDS FOREVER

JONATHAN COTT

University of Minnesota Press
Minneapolis
London

Published by the University of Minnesota Press
111 Third Avenue South, Suite 290
Minneapolis, MN 55401-2520
http://www.upress.umn.edu

ISBN 978-1-5179-1448-6 (hc)
ISBN 978-1-5179-1724-1 (pb)

LC record available at https://lccn.loc.gov/2024000429

Printed in Canada on acid-free paper

The University of Minnesota is an equal-opportunity educator and employer.

30 29 28 27 26 25 24   10 9 8 7 6 5 4 3 2 1

Strawberry Fields is anywhere you want to go.
    —John Lennon, in a 1968 interview with Jonathan Cott

Penny Lane is in my ears and in my eyes
There beneath the blue suburban skies
    —"Penny Lane," Lennon–McCartney

CONTENTS

Paul and John composing "I Saw Her Standing There" in Paul's family home at 20 Forthlin Road in Liverpool, November 1962. Photograph by Mike McCartney, copyright Mike McCartney.

INTRODUCTION

The first time I ever heard "Penny Lane" and "Strawberry Fields Forever" was on February 13, 1967. It all began that morning when I was walking down Benvenue Avenue in Berkeley, California. After having been co-cooned in my apartment for several days writing a lengthy term paper for a graduate school English literature class, I was heading toward the University of California campus to drop it off at my professor's office. It was cool but the sun was up, the sky was blue, and I heard music drifting out of someone's open window—it was loud enough for me to hear it—and it stopped me in my tracks. I stood there and listened. I heard a series of staccato piano chords and a dazzling, soaring solo melody played by a high-pitched trumpet. There was a blur of words, and I could only make out what sounded to me like "Anylane is in my ears and in my eyes / There relief the blue suburban skies," but the voice was unmistakably that of Paul McCartney, and the ecstatic, heart-melting, two-part male harmonies could have been none other than those of McCartney and John Lennon. And then the song was over, and I heard the voice of what I was sure was a radio disc jockey shouting out, "And that's the new Beatles song! It's just out today and it's so great and we've gotta hear it again. Let's hear it again!" I continued to stand there as he played it again, and it was even *better* than great, and this time I heard that "Anylane" was actually "Penny Lane."

A new Beatles song or album was, to me, always a cause for univer-sal jubilation and one that unfailingly buoyed my spirits. But when the

Beatles had released their wondrous album *Rubber Soul* a year earlier, it seemed then as if not just I but the entire world greeted its arrival with joy abounding. I'll never forget walking down the street one morning in January 1966, much as I had done today, and hearing intermingling and overlapping snatches of songs like "Girl," "Norwegian Wood," and "I'm Looking through You" emerging out of a myriad of open windows—the Beatles were the soundtrack of Benvenue Avenue!—but today it was only one Beatles song, "Penny Lane," that was in my ears and in my eyes.

So after I dropped off my term paper, which was about Geoffrey Chaucer's *The Canterbury Tales,* I sped down to a record store on Telegraph Avenue and grabbed one of the two remaining copies of the 45 rpm single of "Penny Lane." It cost a dollar and something, and I was surprised to see that it was enclosed in a unique double-picture cover sleeve that, on one side, showed photographs of the four Beatles as children and, on the other side, a mock-framed color photograph of them, now grown up, no longer the mop-headed Fab Four but now mustachioed and nattily dressed, and seated as if for a formal studio portrait in a gold-embroidered picture frame.

When I got back to my apartment, I gently pulled the record from its sleeve, inserted a small 45 rpm plastic adapter into the record, placed it on my dinky record player's turntable, and listened to McCartney describing the denizens of Penny Lane in the south Liverpool suburb of Mossley Hill, where, under blue suburban skies, we see a barber who's showing photographs of every head he's had the pleasure to know, a banker with a motorcar who never wears a mac, a fireman with an hourglass who likes to keep his fire engine clean, and a bus shelter in the middle of a roundabout where a pretty nurse, who feels as if she's in a play, is selling poppies from a tray—a children's color picture-book world where everyone who comes and goes stops and says hello, evincing what the Cuban writer Alejo Carpentier called "the marvelous real" and what the poet William Wordsworth called "the everyday sublime."

I flipped the record over, and on its B side was a song called "Strawberry Fields Forever." But in fact it wasn't the single's B side. Both Capitol

Records in the United States and Parlophone Records in Great Britain had released "Penny Lane" and "Strawberry Fields Forever" as a double A-side recording, which meant that they couldn't promote one song over the other, nor could one of the songs even be considered first among equals. The Beatles were the first rock group in Great Britain to release double A-side records, but one doesn't know whether they specifically intended to convey that or highlight the contrasting meanings of the songs that they had chosen to mate with each other.

Their first double A-side single, released in 1965, paired "Day Tripper" with "We Can Work It Out." The former song, written primarily by John, is about a "one-way ticket" girl, a "big teaser" who only plays "one night stands." The latter song, written primarily by Paul, is about a long-term relationship in jeopardy of falling apart, and about his hopes to keep its flames alive. The second double A-side single, released in 1966, combined "Eleanor Rigby" and "Yellow Submarine." The former was written by Paul and tells the story, with piercing details, of a lonely spinster and a priest named Father McKenzie who sits alone at night darning his socks. On the flip side was a euphoric children's song, "Yellow Submarine," written primarily by Paul, which is a rock and roll ode to joy about people living an enraptured life together in a kind of love-powered underwater commune.

I didn't know what "Strawberry Fields Forever" had in store for me, but I was going to meet friends for dinner, so I decided to wait until I returned that evening to listen to the "other" A side. I told my friends about the new Beatles single I'd bought that morning, and raved about "Penny Lane"—they were more partial to the Rolling Stones and had equally raved to me a month before about the Stones' new single "Let's Spend the Night Together" and "Ruby Tuesday"—but when they asked me what the other song was like, I said that I'd be listening to it that night.

When I got home, I put "Strawberry Fields Forever" on the record player, and as soon as I heard the first few seconds of a hovering, spectral flute-like melody, I realized that I wasn't in Penny Lane anymore. I could already tell that if "Penny Lane" was like a morning Indian raga, this song was going to be a midnight raga, so I decided to listen to it with the lights out. I lifted the tone arm from the record, started the song from the beginning, lay down on the bed, and closed my eyes.

It was the right thing to do. This was obviously a John song, and in a voice both intimate and faraway he was inviting me—us—to go down with him to a place called Strawberry Fields, where nothing is real and nothing to get hung about. Unlike "Penny Lane," where "brightness falls from the air" (to use a beautiful image by the poet Thomas Nashe), Strawberry Fields was a dark place. The writer Mark Strand tells us in one of his poems that he has a key, so he opens the door and says: "It is dark, and I walk in. / It is darker, and I walk in." John, too, is not afraid to walk deeper into the darkness but admits that "it's getting hard to be someone." He once declared that "Strawberry Fields Forever" was "psychoanalysis set to music," and in this song you observe him free-associating, unpeeling the layers of his identity, as well as delving, scanning, and exploring his own mind as he haltingly sings "Always, no sometimes, think it's me / But you know I know when it's a dream / I think, I know, I mean a 'Yes' / But it's all wrong / That is I think I disagree." In this stanza John uses the word *I* six times and the word *know* three times, with its play on the homonyms *know* and *no*. But there is a yes in there as well, and John tells us that it will all work out. To borrow the title of a book by the psychiatrist Mark Epstein, John is "going to pieces without falling apart."

How amazing, I thought, that "Penny Lane" and "Strawberry Fields Forever" shared the same record. What did they have in common? That question would continue to tantalize me, and it was only years later that I came up with an epiphanic answer when I read a revelatory book titled *The Dream and the Underworld* by the psychologist James Hillman. In it Hillman points out that in Greek mythology Zeus (the god of the sky) and Hades (the god of the underworld) are brothers, and the fact of their brotherhood "indicates that the upper and lower worlds are the same, but only the perspectives differ, one brother viewing things from above and through the light, the other from below and into the darkness." And it dawned on me that Penny Lane is the world of Zeus, and Strawberry Fields the world of Hades. The first is Paul's world, the second is John's—Paul takes you "back" and John takes you "down," but the songs turn out to be two sides of the same coin, the same record.

Just as Zeus and Hades were brothers, so Paul and John were musical brothers-in-arms, but they were also sibling rivals. As the Beatles' producer George Martin told the English journalist Ray Coleman in *Lennon: The Definitive Biography*: "Imagine two people pulling on a rope, smiling at each other and pulling all the time with all their might. The tension between the two of them made for the bond." On November 24, 1966, John had introduced "Strawberry Fields Forever" to his bandmates at Abbey Road Studios, and on December 29, Paul responded with "Penny Lane." "There was amazing competition between us and we both thrived on it," Paul remarked to *Uncut* magazine's Tom Pinnock. "It was a great way for us to keep each other on our toes. I'd write 'Yesterday' and John would go away and write 'Norwegian Wood.' I'd come up with 'Paperback Writer' and John would come back with 'I'm Only Sleeping.' If he wrote 'Strawberry Fields,' it was like he'd upped the ante, so I had to come up with something as good as 'Penny Lane.'" Martin concurred, and as he told *Rolling Stone* in 2001: "'Penny Lane' was generated by a kind of 'I can do just as well as you can, John' because we'd just recorded 'Strawberry Fields.' It was such a knockout that I think Paul went back to perfect his idea. And they were both significant. And they were both about their childhoods."

In "A Hard Day's Nights," the essay following this Introduction, I recount the story of how John and Paul first met. John was almost seventeen and Paul was fifteen. John was playing guitar at an outdoor concert at a church fete in Woolton, a suburb of Liverpool, with his skiffle / rock and roll band, and Paul, who was already a skilled guitarist, was in attendance. I describe how they joined forces as teenagers and became collaborators who, whether they wrote their Beatles songs together or mostly on their own, credited them equally under the conjoined name of Lennon–McCartney. And even after the Beatles broke up, John would acknowledge, "I wouldn't write like I write now if it weren't for Paul, and he wouldn't write like he does if it weren't for me." Neither one of them could read or write music, and as Paul humorously remarked to the *New Yorker*'s John Colapinto, "Someone once told us that the Egyptian pharaohs couldn't read or write—they had scribes to put down their thoughts. So John and I used to say, 'We're like the pharaohs!'"

They also shared the loss of their mothers—Paul's mother died when he was fourteen, John's when he was seventeen. "That became a very big bond between John and me," Paul said in *The Beatles Anthology*. "We both had this emotional turmoil which we had to deal with, and, being teenagers, we had to deal with it very quickly. We both understood that something had happened that you couldn't talk about, but we could laugh about it because each of us had gone through it. It wasn't okay for anyone else. We could both laugh at death, but only on the surface. John went through hell, but young people don't show grief—they'd rather not." Yet Paul would later reveal to Tom Frangione of SiriusXM's *The Beatles Channel* one of those instances when they did: "The night we cried, that was to do with a time when we were in Key West down in Florida, and for some reason—I think it was like a hurricane—something had been delayed, and we couldn't play for a couple of days, so we holed up in a little motel. So what would we do? Well, we'd have a drink, and we would get drunk. We got drunk and started to get kind of emotional. On the way to that, there was a lot of soul-searching. We told each other a few truths, you know, 'Well, I love you,' 'I love you, man,' 'I love that you said that,' and we opened up. So that was kind of special to me. I think that was really one of the only times that ever happened."

But their fraternal relationship also included lengthy periods of misattunement and anger, and after they went their separate musical ways, Paul took a swipe at John in his song "Too Many People," and John returned the favor in his scathing "How Do You Sleep?" It was a far cry from their teenage years, when Paul and John sat on John's bed and played records by Fats Domino, Jerry Lee Lewis, the Everly Brothers, Chuck

Berry, and Buddy Holly. Yet just hours before he died, John told the San Francisco DJ Dave Sholin, "Paul's like a brother. I love him. Families . . . we certainly have our ups and downs and quarrels. But at the end of the day, when it's all said and done, I would do anything for him. I think he would do anything for me."

❖

"Strawberry Fields Forever" and "Penny Lane" were conceived, created, and recorded in 1966—John wrote his song that autumn in Almería, Spain, and Paul wrote his song in November at his home in North London—and they were the culmination of what was probably the most transformative, life-altering, and certainly the most chaotic year in the Beatles' professional lives. In the chapter "A Hard Day's Nights: June–December 1966," I give a detailed account of the onslaught of tumultuous events that they experienced which forced them to fundamentally question who they were and what they wanted to be.

It all began when they flew to Munich, Germany, on June 21 of that year for the first leg of what would turn out to be an apocalyptic two-month, five-country tour during which they received death threats, were physically attacked, had their records burned, and were besieged by hordes of the most frenzied fans they had ever encountered. And I explain how, at its conclusion, the Beatles decided to call it quits to their life as a touring band and redefine themselves solely as recording artists. They also permanently divested themselves of their moptops and their corseting concert uniform—matching collarless onstage suits, skinny black ties, and drainpipe trousers—and began to sport mustaches and beards and to emblazon themselves with vibrantly colorful clothing. No longer wanting to be branded "the Fab Four," they underwent a kind of group identity crisis and took leave from each other for three months, and I chronicle the individuating journeys that they took which were at once physical, psychological, and spiritual.

The Beatles had agreed to return to Abbey Road Studios in late November, and when they did, they immediately began recording "Strawberry Fields Forever" and, afterward, "Penny Lane," one of the most complicated, tortuous, and lengthiest recording sessions ever undertaken by the group. It took more than seventy hours of studio work to create seven minutes of music—"Penny Lane" is just over three minutes, "Strawberry Fields Forever" just over four minutes. Their brevity, however, belies an inexhaustible richness and depth of meaning.

My own abiding fascination with these songs harks back to that morning of February 13, 1967, when I first heard them as I walked past that half-opened apartment window on Benvenue Avenue in Berkeley, and then later that evening as I lay on my bed in my own apartment. In hindsight, it now seems as if I had dreamt them, and as Hillman wrote in *The Dream and the Underworld*: "For a dream image to work in life it must, like a mystery, be experienced as fully real." These songs have been vividly resonating in my imagination for more than a half century, and they have taken me on innumerable journeys down to Strawberry Fields and back to Penny Lane. (In fact, when I went to Liverpool in 1986, I paid a visit to the Cavern Club, where the Beatles first grew their fledgling musical wings.) Thanks to Hillman, I also visited the two songs in the domains of Zeus and Hades, whose perspectives differ even though their upper and lower worlds are ultimately the same, and whose brotherly consanguinity was attested to in the perfect pairing of "Penny Lane" and "Strawberry Fields Forever" on two sides of a 45 rpm record.

Similarly, I decided to conceptualize *Let Me Take You Down* as if it, too, were two sides of a single record. The "first side" of my book sees things from outside and above and describes in detail the events that took place from June to December 1966 which culminated in the conception, creation, and recording of "Penny Lane" and "Strawberry Fields Forever." The "second side" conversely views and examines the songs from inside and below through the perspectives of other persons. In hinging my own interpretation of the two songs on the metaphor of the gods Zeus and

Hades, I thought I had indubitably discovered the nub of the songs, but as Hillman stated: "The depth of even the simplest image is truly fathomless, and this unending, embracing depth is one way that dreams show their love," and he declared: "Dreams call from the imagination to the imagination and can be answered only by the imagination."

I believe that any one person's view of these multifaceted songs can often be narrow, and we need someone else or, even better, several other persons to raise the blinds and help us to discover and even imagine new and more profound ways of seeing—as the French essayist Joseph Joubert remarked: "Imagination is the eye of the soul." In his book *I and Thou* the philosopher Martin Buber wrote: "If we go on our way and meet someone who has advanced towards us and has also gone on *their* way, we know only *our* part of the way, not theirs—theirs we experience only in the meeting." To expand the borders of my journey, and gain new vistas and multiple perspectives on these songs—musical, literary, psychological, cultural, historical, and spiritual—I was fortunate to be able to meet with and engage in a series of conversations that constitute the entire "second side" of my book with five remarkable people: the media artist Laurie Anderson, the guitarist Bill Frisell, the actor Richard Gere, the Jungian analyst Margaret Klenck, and the urban planner, writer, and musician Jonathan F. P. Rose. All of them shared with me their experiences about how these songs intersected with and affected their lives, and in doing so they enabled me to reimagine these songs, hear and listen to them with new ears, understand and think about them with a new mind, and feel them with a reawakened heart. They were my guiding spirits and companions on my journey, and it was by virtue of their insights that I was able to fulfill the promise I had made to myself when I first began to write my book: follow the songs wherever they lead.

A HARD DAY'S NIGHTS

June–December 1966

It was the straw that finally broke the Beatles' back.

On June 24, 1966, the Beatles began what would turn out to be the Tour from Hell. It would take them from West Germany, Japan, and the Philippines, where they performed thirteen concerts in two weeks, to fourteen cities in the United States and Canada, where they performed nineteen open-air concerts from August 12 to August 29.

All the concerts lasted around thirty minutes, and the immutable set-list comprised the following eleven songs:

"Rock and Roll Music" (a Chuck Berry cover)
"She's a Woman"
"If I Needed Someone"
"Day Tripper"
"Baby's in Black"
"I Feel Fine"
"Yesterday"
"I Wanna Be Your Man"
"Nowhere Man"
"Paperback Writer"
"I'm Down" or "Long Tall Sally" (a Little Richard cover)

Their concerts in Munich, Essen, and Hamburg were their first in that country since December 1962, when they played their final engagement at the Star-Club in Hamburg. They had first arrived in that gritty and raunchy port city in August 1960—at that time, Pete Best was the band's drummer (Ringo didn't join until August 1962)—and for two years they served their musical apprenticeship in the red-light district, wearing their black-leather outfits and cowboy boots and playing four to six sets for four to five hours every night at clubs on the Reeperbahn and Große Freiheit street, honing their performance skills and living an unrestrained, Preludin-fueled rock and roll lifestyle. In *The Beatles Anthology*, a book that presents the history of the Beatles in their own words, John explained: "I might have been born in Liverpool but I grew up in Hamburg"; Paul remarked: "We all got our education in Hamburg"; and George declared: "I'd have to say with hindsight that Hamburg bordered on the best of the Beatles times. We didn't have any luxury, we didn't have any bathrooms or any clothes, we were pretty grubby, we couldn't afford anything, but on the other hand we weren't yet famous, so we didn't have to contend with the bullshit that comes with fame." But they were now returning four years later as world-conquering heroes, and like everywhere else they were greeted by screaming teenagers—most of them girls—at the airports, outside their hotels, and in the concert halls. Several girls were said to have torn off their clothes at one concert, and a West German newspaper reported that even two overwrought boys had to be carried away at another one after having lost consciousness. As the guitarist Lenny Kaye remarks in his book *Lightning Striking: Ten Transformative Moments in Rock and Roll*, "Each Beatle takes his turn in the limelight and you are overtaken by their combined synergy. Especially since they're now used to the adulation, playing it like another instrument. The screams may be predominantly female, but the guys look under the hood, at the way the engine is sparking."

The tour began in Munich, and the Beatles arrived there on June 23, two days after having completed their recording sessions at Abbey Road

Studios—known at that time as EMI Recording Studios—for one of their greatest albums, *Revolver,* which includes masterpieces such as "Eleanor Rigby," "Here, There and Everywhere," "She Said She Said," and "I'm Only Sleeping," none of which they performed on the tour. Their first two concerts took place the following day at the 3,500-seat Circus-Krone-Bau. The band was tired and unrehearsed, forgot some of the lyrics, and occasionally sang out of tune, but no one stood up and walked out on them; few in the audience noticed or cared because the cascade of shrieks and screams drowned out the music, and all that mattered was that the band was back where they once belonged. But as a presage of the violence that would unabatedly wreak havoc on this tour, rampaging street thugs outside the theater smashed windows and overturned cars and were subjected to beatings and tear gas by police with guard dogs.

The Beatles arrived in Tokyo on June 30, where they were scheduled to play a grueling five shows over three days. The venue for their performances was the Nippon Budokan arena, which had previously been reserved for sumo wrestling and martial arts, and memorial ceremonies for the Japanese war dead are held there annually. Unbeknownst to the Beatles, two weeks before their arrival ultranationalist students and members of the Greater Japan Patriotic Party, outraged by the impending desacralization and defilement of what they considered a sacred space, had begun staging street protests, urging people to "shave the Beatles' long hair," and plastered thousands of posters along Tokyo's main streets reading "Beatles Go Home" and "Beat Away the Beatles from Japan," and they vowed to disrupt the concerts. The Beatles received death threats, and in one of the largest security operations ever carried out in Japan, more than eight thousand police officers—from police detectives to snipers—and a fire brigade were mobilized to protect the group during its stay in Tokyo. About three thousand white-gloved police officers encircled the band during concerts, and the ground-floor seating had been cleared; only balcony seats were sold, and concertgoers were instructed not to stand, dance, or leave their seats. The concerts went off peacefully, but between performances the Beatles were confined to the presidential suite of the Tokyo Hilton, essentially under house arrest. It is significant that the group's concerts at Budokan broke the ice for future groups touring Japan to perform there, and as the journalist Steve McClure wrote in the *Japan Times,* the Beatles' five shows at Budokan had "conferred on it a quasi-sacred status in rock mythology."

On the next leg of their journey into the Inferno, the Beatles flew from Tokyo to Manila on July 3, and when they landed at the airport, there were about ten thousand fans at its perimeter—surrounded by police officers, motorcyclists, armored cars, fire trucks, and riot squad jeeps— waiting to greet them, but the welcoming signs they carried should have read "Abandon all hope, ye who enter here." As the band disembarked from the plane, armed men in civilian clothes—the Beatles described them as "thugs"—suddenly rushed up and yelled "Leave those bags there!" and whisked them into the back of a vehicle. "Everyone had guns," Ringo commented in *The Beatles Anthology,* "and it was really like that hot/ Catholic/gun/Spanish Inquisition attitude."

The Beatles were driven to the Philippine Navy Headquarters, facing the city's marina, where they participated in an unplanned press conference in the war room. Without any foreknowledge, they were then led out the back entrance to a private luxury yacht that was anchored in the Manila Harbor and which was owned by a wealthy Filipino industrialist whose twenty-four-year-old son, who had recently graduated magna cum laude from Harvard, was hosting a party to show off the Beatles to his friends. "It was really humid, it was Mosquito City," George recalled in *The Beatles Anthology,* "and we were all sweating and frightened. For the first time in our Beatle existence, we were cut off from Neil, Mal, and Brian Epstein. [Epstein was the Beatles' manager, and Neil Aspinall and Mal Evans were their road managers.] There was not one of them around, and not only that, but we had a whole row of cops with guns lining the deck around this cabin we were in on the boat. We were really gloomy, very brought down by the whole thing. We wished we hadn't come here."

The Filipino host had planned for the Beatles to remain on the yacht until the following day, but Epstein arrived and had them driven to the Manila Hotel, where they arrived at 4:30 a.m. But a few hours later they became embroiled in what would turn out to be a political, diplomatic, and personal nightmare. Unbeknownst to them, Imelda Marcos, nicknamed the Iron Butterfly and the wife of the country's dictator, Ferdinand Marcos, had organized a well-publicized reception at the Malacañang Palace for the morning of July 4—five hours before the first of the Beatles' two concerts—to which around three hundred children of the government elite and senior military personnel had been invited to meet the Beatles. Epstein had previously turned down the first lady's request while they were still in Japan, but word of that had not gotten through to the palace. So when a fleet of government limousines and motorcyclists showed up at the Manila Hotel at 10 a.m. to escort the band to the palace, the Beatles were asleep. Two colonels from the Manila police and Philippine Constabulary went up to the fourth-floor suite, banged on the door, and tried to persuade the Beatles to come to the palace. Epstein was in the room, and according to the *Philippines Free Press,* he told them, "If *they* want to see the Beatles, let them come here," and when one colonel informed him that the "they" included Ferdinand Marcos, one of the Beatles said, "Who he?" The limousines left empty-handed.

The Beatles gave a late afternoon and an evening concert at the Rizal Memorial Football Stadium to a combined audience of eighty thousand people—"The sound was terrible, the Beatles were terrific," wrote one newspaper reviewer, although another reporter called the performances "listless"—but during the four hours separating those concerts state television was broadcasting scenes of weeping children at the palace, with shots of the four empty seats reserved for the no-show Beatles and Imelda Marcos screaming "They've let me down!" The next morning newspapers carried headlines like IMELDA STOOD UP: FIRST FAMILY WAITS IN VAIN FOR MOPTOPS AT THE PRESIDENTIAL PALACE.

All hell broke loose. The nation was enraged, the Beatles received death threats, the Philippine promoter refused to pay the Beatles for their performances, police and security for the Beatles were withdrawn, the hotel staff disappeared, and the Beatles had to carry their own luggage, musical instruments, and amplifiers and order their own cabs to the Manila International Airport, which one of the Beatles described as an "armed military camp." When they got out of the cabs, hundreds of livid Filipinos lined the path into the terminal building and heckled and harangued them, and at the airport people started spitting at them, so Ringo and John spotted a group of nuns and hid behind them because Ringo knew that since this was a Catholic country, the mob wouldn't attack the nuns. On the instructions of the airport manager, Willy Jurado, the escalators had been turned off, and when the Beatles finally arrived in the departure lounge, uniformed men and some of the thugs who had greeted them at the airport upon their arrival began kicking and beating them and even injured members of the Beatles entourage. Jurado would later gleefully brag to an American journalist about having knocked Epstein to the ground and then kicking and punching John and Ringo in the face, declaring: "I really thumped them . . . They were pleading like frightened chickens. That's what happens when you insult the First Lady."

Upon their return to London Ringo described to the press their ordeal in Manila as the most frightening thing that ever happened to them, Paul accused their attackers of being cowards, John scribbled on a copy of the tour itinerary "Nearly fucking killed by the Government . . . and it's just another Beatles day," and when questioned by a reporter's question about their long-term plans, George replied: "We're going to have a couple of weeks to recuperate before we go and get beaten up by the Americans."

Four months earlier, the English journalist Maureen Cleave had written an article about John for the March 4 issue of the London *Evening Standard* in which he declared: "Christianity will go. It will vanish and shrink. I needn't argue about that; I know I'm right and I will be proved right. We're more popular than Jesus now. I don't know which will go first—rock 'n' roll or Christianity. Jesus was all right, but his disciples were thick and ordinary. It's them twisting it that ruins it for me." The British media paid little heed to John's statement, and Cleave's article was later syndicated to overseas publications (including the *New York Times*) with nary a reaction.

But just two weeks before the Beatles were to perform their first American concert in Chicago on August 12, the American teen magazine *Datebook* resurrected and reprinted John's remarks in the issue that appeared on newsstands in mid-July, and all heaven broke loose. Within hours of the magazine going on sale, radio station WAQY in Birmingham, Alabama, announced an immediate ban of all Beatles records—radio station KZEE in Weatherford, Texas, went further and "damned their songs eternally"—and scores of radio stations, and not only in the Bible Belt, followed suit. Beatles 45s and LPs were smashed live on the air, and people zealously burned them in bonfires and oil drums at large public gatherings. The South Carolina Grand Dragon of the Ku Klux Klan nailed Beatles albums to a cross and set them aflame at a "Beatle Bonfire" in Chester, and Pastor Thurman H. Babbs of the New Heaven Baptist Church in Cleveland, Ohio, threatened to revoke the membership of any member of his congregation who attended a Beatles concert. And Reno's radio station KCBN broadcast an anti-Beatles editorial every hour.

Back in London, John was remorseful, telling his friends, "How am I to face the others if this whole tour is called off just because of something I said?" So when the Beatles arrived in Chicago he agreed to appear, with Paul, George, and Ringo beside him for moral support, at a press conference at the Astor Tower Hotel to make his confession—but one garnished with a few Lennon twists—stating: "I wasn't saying the Beatles are better than Jesus or God or Christianity . . . I'm not anti-God, anti-Christ, or anti-religion. . . . I was using the name Beatles 'cause I can talk about Beatles as a separate thing and use them as an example, especially to a close friend. But I could have said TV, or cinema, or anything else that's popular . . . or *motorcars* are bigger than Jesus. But I just said Beatles because that's the easiest one for me. . . . I don't profess to be a practising

Christian, and Christ was what he was and anything anybody says great about him I believe. I'm not a practising Christian, but I don't have any un-Christian thoughts. . . . But I said it in that way, which was the wrong way, yap, yap. . . . I'm sorry I opened my mouth."

The Lennon apology placated a number of radio stations, which lifted their bans, and some previously vitriolic journalists tempered their wrath, so Epstein decided that the tour could continue. But the diehard critics remained unforgiving, the Beatles were still receiving death threats, and before they exited their plane at the Memphis International Airport on August 19 for their two shows at the Mid-South Coliseum, George joked that they should send John out first, and John grimly remarked, "You might just as well paint a target on me." On their way into the city they were greeted by young protesters waving placards proclaiming BEATLES GO HOME and JESUS DIED FOR YOU, TOO, JOHN LENNON, but even with a security detail of some eighty police officers, it was necessary for decoy limousines to be sent ahead while the Beatles rode in a specially outfitted bus, huddled on the floor to protect themselves from potential snipers. A local preacher staged a rally outside the Coliseum, and six members of the Ku Klux Klan picketed close by, attired in their white hoods and robes. Inside, as the Beatles press officer Tony Barrow later recalled in his memoir *John, Paul, George, Ringo & Me,* a cherry bomb firecracker was thrown onto the stage during the second concert when John was singing "Nowhere Man"—John fearlessly shouted out "this song's for you" to the perpetrator—and, as Barrow wrote, "all of us at the side of the stage, including the three Beatles onstage, looked immediately at John Lennon. We would not at that moment have been surprised to see that guy go down."

There were no protests when the Beatles played at Cleveland's Municipal Stadium on August 14, but for the first time during the tour, Beatle fans ran rampant. As the band sang "Day Tripper," more than 2,500 people broke through the security barriers and stormed the stage while the police futilely attempted to ward them off. The Beatles had to stop playing and take shelter backstage, and after reappearing half an hour later and finishing the eleven-song set, they quickly rushed off-stage, and as they did, the unrelenting fans once again rushed the stage and attempted to take sound equipment and instruments as souvenirs. The *Plain Dealer* reported: "Over the years there has been a lot of activity around second base at Cleveland Stadium. But even with all the hundreds of sporting events that have taken place on that section of lakefront real estate, never has there been activity like there was last night." Barrow called the concert "one of the wildest shows" of the tour.

But the crowd mayhem at the Beatles' concert at Dodger Stadium in Los Angeles on August 28 proved to be even more shambolic. As soon as the band finished playing, about seven thousand people broke through the fencing and impeded the Beatles from leaving the stadium, and in his memoir Barrow described the insanity that ensued when hundreds of maniacal fans surrounded the getaway car and began to climb over it. The car sped backward across the field at breakneck speed, and people flung themselves out of its way, but even this failed to clear a path for the band's escape, so the driver headed for a dugout at the far side of the field. The Beatles rushed out of the car, raced underground, and for two hours they were trapped in a team dressing room while extra police came in to start clearing the mob. The getaway car was severely damaged, and two girls ran off with the ignition key as a souvenir. "All four boys were on the point of despair," Barrow writes, "and we were discussing the possibility that our party might have to stay cooped up at the stadium overnight. Ringo broke the ensuing silence by saying in a small voice: 'Can I please go home to my mummy now, please can I?'" Three attempts to escape using decoy limousines failed, and "finally we were put into an ambulance that managed to crash into a heap of broken fencing, after which it couldn't be driven any further. Extra squads of police from the sheriff's department eventually escorted us away in an armored car. Silently to ourselves we repeated Ringo's heartfelt plea. We wanted to go home now. Please, could we?"

All of them seemed to share his sentiment. Ringo complained that they were turning into bad musicians, that no one was listening at the shows, that he couldn't hear anything when they were playing, and as he remarked in the film *Eight Days a Week: The Touring Years*: "I'd be watching John's arse, or Paul's arse, his foot tapping, his head nodding to see where we were in the song." In any case, most audiences wouldn't have been able to judge the quality of the performances because the music couldn't be amplified loud enough to compete with screaming crowds. At the Beatles' legendary August 15, 1965, concert at Shea Stadium in Queens, New York, which was attended by more than fifty-five thousand fans, the decibel level was calculated to have been 131.35 decibels, which would have been 28 decibels louder than a jumbo jet flying one hundred feet overhead. One attendee declared: "The music? Didn't hear it. Didn't matter. I was there." On this occasion, however, John, standing on a stage just off second base, was uplifted by the experience, saying to the concert's promoter Sid Bernstein, "You know, Sid, at Shea Stadium I saw the top of the mountain."

But for John those peak experiences were becoming fewer and farther between. In his biography *John Lennon* Philip Norman quotes him as saying: "I reckon we could send out four waxwork dummies of ourselves and that would satisfy the crowds. Beatles concerts are nothing to do with music anymore. They're just bloody tribal rituals." John also recounted to the London *Daily Mirror*'s columnist Donald Zec the disturbing story that on the Beatles' first American tour "theater managers kept bringing blind . . . children into our dressing room. This boy's mother would say to us, 'Go on, kiss him, maybe you'll bring back his sight.' . . . But we're entertainers not faith healers, and if you flinch they snarl at you, want to half murder you. We're not cruel. We've seen enough tragedy in Merseyside. But when a mother shrieks, 'Just touch him! Maybe he'll walk again,' we want to run, cry, empty our pockets. . . . We're going to remain normal if it kills us." Moreover, he said, "I didn't want to tour again, especially after having been accused of crucifying Jesus when all I made was a flippant remark, and having to stand with the Klan outside and firecrackers going on inside. I couldn't take it anymore."

George, too, was fed up and complained that in every city where the Beatles performed they were subject to police control and on the receiving end of a continual barrage of threats; were hermetically confined to hotel rooms, cars, and planes; and although they managed to mitigate the stress with their characteristically buoyant and absurdist sense of humor, enough was enough.

Paul, however, believed that musicians should play live for their fans and had always wanted to keep touring. But his road to Damascus moment occurred on August 21 at Busch Stadium in St. Louis, Missouri. It was pouring rain, the band was protected only by a thin sheet of corrugated tin, the wind was blowing hard, the water was slopping over the stage, and they were afraid it would blow up the amps. And at that moment Paul finally agreed with his mates that enough was really enough.

On the afternoon of August 29, the day after their Dodger Stadium nightmare, the Beatles flew to San Francisco to play the final concert of the American tour at Candlestick Park before an audience of twenty-five thousand people. The five-foot-high stage sat just over second base, and the band started performing the thirty-three-minute set at 9:27 p.m. No one but they knew that this would be their last public concert. To mark the occasion, Paul asked Barrow to make a recording of the concert on his hand-held cassette recorder as a personal souvenir of what he knew would be a historic evening, so Barrow made his way onto the field, stood in the space between the stage and the stands, far enough away from the nonstop screams of the fans, and held up the mike. But the cassette tape, which lasted thirty minutes on each side, ran out in the middle of "Long Tall Sally," which was the concert's concluding song, and he was unable to flip the tape over to the other side in time. Barrow gave the tape to Paul and made a copy for himself, but it has widely circulated as a bootleg. ("We never did identify the music thief," Barrow writes in his memoir.)

Knowing that this would be their touring-life swan song, each of the Beatles brought a camera, took pictures of the crowd, then placed the cameras on top of the amplifiers. Before one of the last songs Ringo got down off the drums, and the four of them turned around and took snap-shots of the unattended stage. Accounts of this differ, but it has also been reported that their roadie, Mal Evans, took a wide-angle-lens photo of all four of them standing at the front of stage with their backs to the audi-ence. They had everything they needed, they were artists, but for one final moment they wanted to look back.

When the exhausted and battle-scarred Beatles returned to England on August 31, they found themselves welcomed and exalted beyond mea-sure. As Steve Turner noted in his book *Beatles '66: The Revolutionary Year*, this would be the last time they would fly back home together and be greeted by screaming fans. Their album *Revolver*, which they had com-pleted recording on June 21—two days before they flew to Munich for the first leg of their Tour from Hell—and which had been released in the United Kingdom on August 5, was now at the top of the UK LP charts; and their double A-side single, "Eleanor Rigby" / "Yellow Submarine," which had been simultaneously released on the same day as *Revolver*, was the number one single.

In his book *Revolution in the Head: The Beatles' Records and the Six-ties*, the English journalist Ian MacDonald, writing about *Revolver*, stated: "The Beatles had initiated a second pop revolution—one which while galvanizing their existing rivals and inspiring many new ones, left all of them far behind." According to *Hit Parader* magazine, *Revolver* repre-sented "the pinnacle of pop music. No group has been as consistently creative as the Beatles. . . . Rather than analyze the music, we just suggest that you listen to *Revolver* three or four times a day and marvel." In *The Rolling Stone Album Guide* Rob Sheffield commented that *Revolver* found the Beatles "at the peak of their powers, competing with one another because nobody else could touch them," and described it as "the best album the Beatles ever made, which means the best album by anybody."

And in his 1968 book *High Priest,* Timothy Leary vertiginously proposed that the Beatles were "Divine Messiahs, the wisest, holiest, most effective avatars that the human race has yet produced ... prototypes of a new race of laughing freemen. Evolutionary agents sent by God, endowed with mysterious power to create a new human species."

Just a few hours after their farewell concert in San Francisco, the Beatles had boarded an airplane to Los Angeles from where they would fly to London, and George announced: "That's it, I'm not a Beatle anymore!" He meant that he was no longer a "touring" Beatle, but he was relieved that he would no longer have to deal with all the craziness. For John, however, the prospect of no longer touring initially triggered extreme anxiety. "I couldn't deal with not being continually onstage," he later admitted to *Newsweek*'s Barbara Graustark. "That was the first time I thought, My God, what do you do if this isn't going on? What else is there?"

"I live on Earth at present," the American architect R. Buckminster Fuller wrote in his book *I Seem to Be a Verb,* "and I don't know what I am. I know I am not a category. I am not a thing—a noun. I seem to be a verb, an evolutionary process—an integral function of the Universe." Substitute the word *Beatle* for the words *category* and *thing,* and it's clear that the Beatles no longer wanted to be nouns. The philosopher Friedrich Nietzsche declared, "Become what you are," and each of the Beatles would now begin the evolutionary process of becoming verbs. "What would it be like *not* to be a Beatle?" and "What would you *be* if you weren't a Beatle?" were the questions that John, Paul, and George asked themselves. And they decided to find out.

In her Neapolitan novel *Those Who Leave and Those Who Stay,* Elena Ferrante writes: "The better and truer you feel, the farther away you go." Ringo decided to stay home with his wife and child and cultivate his garden, but the other three Beatles decided to go away. After agreeing to reconvene at Abbey Road Studios at the end of November, they took leave of each other for three months and, disguising themselves as best as they could with mustaches, beards, short haircuts, and sunglasses, they left England. George went to India, John went to Germany and Spain, and Paul, after staying in London for a month, took a solitary road trip in France.

George was the first to leave. On September 14, two weeks after having returned to England, he and his wife, Pattie, flew to Mumbai (then known as Bombay) in order to have sitar lessons with the great sitar master Ravi Shankar. Before George left London, Shankar had written him a letter in which he advised: "Try to disguise yourself—couldn't you grow a mustache?" So George grew a mustache and had his hair cut short, and when he and Pattie arrived in Mumbai they checked in to the Taj Mahal Palace hotel under the names Mr. and Mrs. Sam Wells. They began wearing Indian kurtas, and George wore wire-rimmed sunglasses so that when they walked around the city, they remained unrecognized. But their freedom was short-lived, because after a week of blissful anonymity, an elevator operator at the hotel saw through their disguises and blew their cover. An English-language newspaper headlined its disclosure article BY GEORGE—A BEATLE IS IN TOWN, and George was pressured to give a press conference in which he explained: "I am here not as a Beatle, I have come as plain George Harrison to learn the sitar and something of Indian classical music. I have what may be termed a Beatle's life, and a private life. It isn't always easy to separate the two. My growing interest in the culture of the East belongs to the latter."

George had first become enamored of the sitar when the Beatles were filming their second feature film, *Help!,* in April 1965. "We were waiting to shoot the scene in the restaurant when the guy gets thrown in the soup," George later recounted to *Billboard* magazine, "and there were a few Indian musicians playing in the background. I remember picking up the sitar and trying to hold it and thinking, 'This is a funny sound.' It was an incidental thing, but somewhere down the line I began to hear Ravi Shankar's name, and the third time I heard it, I thought, 'This is an odd coincidence.' I went and bought a Ravi record, and I put it on, and it hit a certain spot in me that I can't explain, but it seemed familiar to me. The only way I could describe it was: my intellect didn't know what was going on and yet this other part of me identified with it. It just called on me." And as he told Maureen Cleave, he had become so smitten with the music that before going to sleep at night he fantasized about what it would be like to actually be inside one of Shankar's sitars.

George made some inchoate attempts to play the sitar, and he played it on the Beatles' song "Norwegian Wood (This Bird Has Flown)," which was included on their 1965 album *Rubber Soul,* and it was the first time the sitar had been used on a Western rock recording. (A year later, the Rolling Stones featured it on their song "Paint It Black," and two years later the English group Traffic used it on their song "Paper Sun.") George had at first shied away from meeting Shankar, but they finally did so in early June 1966, when the founder of the Asian Music Circle invited both of them for dinner at his London home. "From the moment we met," Shankar told the *Guardian* in 1999, "George was asking questions, and I felt he was genuinely interested in Indian music and religion. He appeared to be a sweet, straightforward young man. I said I had been told he had used the sitar, although I had not heard the song 'Norwegian Wood.' He seemed quite embarrassed, and it transpired that he had only had a few sittings with an Indian chap who was in London to see how the instrument should be held and to learn the basics of playing."

Six months later, George was in Mumbai, and Shankar visited him in his suite at the Taj Mahal Palace to begin teaching him the instrument in earnest, and Shankar brought in a yoga teacher who gave George exercises that would enable him to play more comfortably in what was for him the painful traditional half-lotus posture; and the teacher also introduced George to Vedic meditation techniques.

Because George could no longer disguise himself as Mr. Wells, and because his sitar lessons would be difficult to continue in Mumbai, Shankar decided to take George and Pattie on a cross-country pilgrimage, which George described as "the privileged tour." They visited the Ajanta Caves—Buddhist temples, prayer halls, and monasteries cut into the side of a volcanic cliff—and Shankar took them to the holy city of Benares, where the Ramlila festival was then taking place; and here, along with thousands of pilgrims and ash-smeared and dreadlocked Hindu holy men called sadhus, they witnessed the dramatic folk reenactment of the god Rama. In the city of Maihar, Shankar introduced them to Baba Allauddin Khan, his then-104-year-old guru, master sarod player, and one of the twentieth century's most famous teachers of Indian classical music. The culmination of the journey was Kashmir, where they stayed on houseboats on Dal Lake, near Srinagar, with lotus flowers and lily pads in full bloom and the snow-covered Himalayas in the distance. Close to one of the houseboats was a Mughal-era garden with centuries-old chinar trees, and under them George and Shankar would sit together in the afternoons, and George would spend hours studiously practicing Indian scales along with his teacher.

George and John Lennon took their first LSD trip together in April 1965, and while they were on the drug George heard the words "Yogis of the Himalayas." That image haunted him, and he realized that the reason for his wanting to go to India was not only to get lessons from Ravi Shankar but also to connect to what was for him a new spiritual tradition. "Ravi was my link to the Vedic world," he said in *The Beatles Anthology.* "Ravi plugged me into the whole of reality. Elvis impressed me when I was a kid and impressed me when I met him . . . but you couldn't later go round to him and say, 'Elvis, what's happening with the universe?'" George felt that he might have possibly had a past life in India and confessed that his six-week sojourn there was "the first feeling I'd ever had of being liberated from being a Beatle or a number." And in Martin Scorsese's film *Living in the Material World,* he declared: "One by one we get awakened by the sound of Krishna's flute. His flute works in many ways."

Meanwhile, back in London Paul had agreed to compose the soundtrack for a film called *The Family Way,* which depicted the marital troubles of a newlywed working-class couple living in Lancashire. The film was directed by the brothers Roy and John Boulting and starred John

Mills and his daughter Hayley Mills, and it was the first time that the Lennon–McCartney credit wasn't used for a McCartney composition. In fact, Paul's contribution to the soundtrack was minimal. He wrote fifteen seconds of music for the film's main theme, which the Beatles' producer George Martin expanded and arranged for various instruments. The film also required a love theme, and Martin kept pestering Paul to write one but to no avail, so he finally had to go over to Paul's house and stand in his music studio and threaten to write the tune himself until Paul composed what Martin described as "a sweet little fragment of a waltz tune" that they called "Love in the Open Air." Paul played it to Martin on the guitar, and Martin wrote it down and created thirteen versions of this melody, which he arranged for woodwinds and strings—and, at Paul's suggestion, added a brass band—and then used those versions to score the entire film. (Paul received an Ivor Novello Award for Best Instrumental Theme.)

Now that he was a free man in London, Paul enthusiastically reimmersed himself in London's vibrant avant-garde music, literature, and art scene. He had been introduced to it in August 1965, when he met the artist and gallerist John Dunbar, the singer Peter Asher, and the writer Barry Miles (known simply as "Miles") who were in the process of founding the legendary Indica Bookshop and Gallery. Paul was then dating Asher's sister, Jane, and was living at the Ashers' family house on Wimpole Street. From the outset, Paul was a hands-on visitor to Indica in Mason's Yard, which was just then being shelved, painted, and carpeted, and whenever he found the time, he would go there before it officially opened in February 1966 to saw wood, fill in holes and cracks in the plaster walls, and paint them white. He also helped draw the flyers used to advertise the Indica's opening, and even designed the shop's wrapping paper.

Miles and his then wife, Sue, met Paul at Wimpole Street and befriended him, and Paul would frequently visit their Hanson Street apartment, which was a treasure trove of books and records, and Miles introduced him to the works of writers like William Burroughs, Allen Ginsberg, and Lawrence Ferlinghetti, all of whom Miles had met, and to albums by jazz musicians such as John Coltrane, Albert Ayler, Sun Ra, and Ornette Coleman, and composers like Karlheinz Stockhausen, John Cage, and Luciano Berio, and Sue baked and introduced him to his first hash brownie using a recipe called "Hashish Fudge" from *The Alice B. Toklas Cookbook*. Paul spent many intoxicating and hyperinspired evenings in Miles's living room discussing and throwing around all kinds of far-out ideas, and when he would later tell John about them and mentioned that one of his ideas was to make an album titled *Paul McCartney Goes Too Far,* John would say to him, "Fantastic! Do it! Do it!"

Miles and Paul had often talked about the possibility of creating a small demo studio where poets and avant-garde musicians could record their work and exchange and share their tapes with each other and release the most interesting tapes on a small record label on a monthly or semi-annual basis. (Miles would eventually supervise unreleased spoken-word recordings by writers such as Richard Brautigan, Charles Bukowski, Ginsberg, Michael McClure, and Ferlinghetti for Apple Records' short-lived Zapple label.) Paul didn't want to undertake the creation of an expensive recording studio, but he hit upon the idea of renting an apartment that Ringo owned on Montagu Square, and in early 1966 he turned the basement into a mini recording studio. He had intended it to be a place where poets and musicians could create spoken-word and avant-garde musical works, but it was mainly used by Burroughs and one of his friends, the electronics technician Ian Sommerville, and they experimented with backward tapes, superimposed recordings made at different speeds, and created aural cutups from Burroughs's spoken texts and also a variety of radio broadcasts, and then randomly juxtaposed them to reveal and conjure new associations.

Paul occasionally stopped by to observe what Burroughs was doing and engaged in numerous conversations with him about his cutup technique. Paul himself toyed with the idea of experimenting with tape cutups, just as he had done with tape loops for *Revolver,* but he finally decided that the studio should have a more practical use, so he began to use it to make demos for his own songs, one of which was "Eleanor Rigby." Burroughs witnessed the song taking shape and told Paul how impressed he was by how much narrative he was able to compress into three verses. "Paul would come in and work on his 'Eleanor Rigby,'" Burroughs informed his biographer Victor Bockris, "and Ian recorded Paul's rehearsals so I saw the song taking shape. Once again, not knowing much about music, I could see he knew what he was doing. He was very pleasant and prepossessing. Nice-looking young man, hardworking." But soon realizing that the studio was being underused, Paul dismantled it and gave up the flat, and Ringo would eventually rent it to John and Yoko Ono in September 1968, just four months after they officially became a couple.

Paul was also enthusiastic about Miles's idea to create an underground newspaper called *International Times,* and with financial help from Paul, Miles and a number of his writer and activist friends published the first issue in October 1966. Also known as *IT,* the newspaper's mission was to cover stories that the mainstream media overlooked or denigrated, and which would, as Steve Turner encapsulated it, "bring together like-minded people who'd previously existed in isolated pockets—avant-garde artists, recreational drug users, anarchists, old bohemians, New Left political activists, beatniks, Campaign for Nuclear Disarmament campaigners, satirists, feminists, New Age believers, alternative therapists, mind expansionists, vegetarians. What united these people was a general belief in freedom, peace, love, diversity, and tolerance, along with an irritation with conformity, dullness, authority, dead tradition, meaningless routine, and fear of experiment." As Miles proclaimed in the underground newspaper *LongHair Times,* a forerunner of *IT*: "Pipe dreams need no longer be only dreams. Let's make this thing HAPPEN so all may SEE & HEAR." It was a sentiment straight out of the Beatles' playbook.

In his song "Got to Get You into My Life," which appeared on *Revolver,* Paul sang about his desire to take a car ride alone on a new road. In early November 1966 he decided to follow his own advice and, just as George had done when he went to India, not be a Beatle for awhile. His plan was to drive unaccompanied and incognito, with no booked accommodations, from Paris to Bordeaux, check into small hotels, register under a false name, have dinner alone, and not be recognized. To that end, several weeks before his departure for France, he asked a company called Wig Creations to make a theatrical mustache for him that matched the color of his hair, and he bought a pair of clear-lens glasses, a long blue overcoat, a Kodak 8mm movie camera, several journal notebooks, and arranged to have his new dark-green Aston Martin DB5 flown from Lydd Airport to France by a superfreighter air ferry on November 6. He accompanied the car, and after passing through French customs, he immediately glued on his mustache, put on his glasses, slicked back his hair with Vaseline, donned his overcoat, and drove to Paris.

He spent the next five days driving at his own speed through the Loire Valley to Bordeaux, stopping off at chateaux and filming scenes along the way, fancying himself a lonely Romantic poet riding along, like Chuck Berry, in his automobile, and in each town he visited he would walk around unrecognized, take photographs, buy some antiques, and make himself understood as best he could with only phrase-book French; and he would stop overnight in small hotels, register under a false name, and then go up to his room to write in his journal.

Paul had arranged to meet up with his roadie Mal Evans in Bordeaux on November 12 under the clock on the Church of Saint-Éloi, but he arrived in the city a day earlier. He felt like going to a dance club that evening, but when he showed up at the entrance they looked at him as if he had never been born. So he went back to the hotel and then returned to the club looking like "him" and received a reception worthy of a Beatle. It was then that he decided to give up his disguise.

In his book *Playing and Reality,* the English psychoanalyst D. W. Winnicott wrote: "It is a joy to be hidden, but disaster not to be found," and the now-undisguised Paul continued his journey with Evans for another two weeks, traveling through Spain and then flying with him to Kenya to go on a three-day safari. Paul had wanted to be found, but he had also been profoundly affected by his experience of being hidden, and from that experience he got the idea of creating a new identity for the Beatles; and it was during the long flight back from Nairobi to London, throughout which he stayed awake, that he experienced a midair creative lightning bolt and envisioned the idea for *Sgt. Pepper's Lonely Hearts Club Band.* John, George, Ringo, and he would shed their Beatles identities, create alter egos, and transmogrify themselves into a new and born-again band. In a sense, this idea is what the theater director Peter Brook had in mind when he suggested in a 1981 *Parabola* magazine interview that a mask can liberate you by taking away your habitual forms, and the fact that it gives you something to hide behind makes it unnecessary for you to hide. "The fundamental paradox that exists in all acting," Brook explained, "is that because you are in safety, you can go into danger. Because there is a greater security, you can take greater risks, and because here it is *not* you, and therefore everything about you is hidden, you can let yourself appear."

Paul arrived back in London on November 20, and on the evening of December 6 the Sgt. Pepper's Lonely Hearts Club Band "appeared" at Abbey Road Studios and began recording Paul's "When I'm Sixty-Four," whose tune he had composed when he was sixteen years old in Liverpool and which he now revived with sly and whimsical lyrics for what would turn out to be one of the most revolutionary albums in rock and roll history.

John was at loose ends. The Beatles' touring days were over, and never again would they appear together as the moptopped Fab Four in their matching suits. George was on his way to India; Paul would be composing the soundtrack for the film *The Family Way* and exploring the exhilarating London avant-garde music, art, and literary world; and Ringo and his wife, Maureen, and their then-one-year-old son Zak were staying put at his estate in Weybridge, Surrey. Only John was up in the air. Touring had become anathema to him, but he now admitted that he didn't know what to do with himself when he wasn't onstage, and he began to exhibit incipient signs of an identity crisis. Philip Norman quotes John's friend, the art designer and bassist Klaus Voormann, who had designed the album cover for *Revolver*, as saying: "John had gone from pretending to be this tough rock-'n'-roller into being a Beatle, which was also all about pretending. With all that he had, he wasn't happy because he hadn't come to terms with his own personality. He was a Beatle, and he knew that a Beatle doesn't really exist." But as John told Hunter Davies, the author of *The Beatles: The Authorised Biography*, "I have to see the others to see myself. I have to see them to establish contact with myself and come down. Sometimes I don't come down."

Davies writes that shortly after John had returned from California to his Kenwood mansion in Weybridge, Surrey, he had a conversation with his wife, Cynthia, who asked him if he, she, and their son, Julian, could all take a holiday without the Beatles. "Not even with our Beatle buddies?" John asked. "It's nice to have your mates around." And Cynthia told him, "They seem to need you less than you need them." "We do need each other a lot," John confessed to Davies. "When we used to meet again after a month off, we used to be embarrassed about touching each other. We'd do an elaborate handshake just to hide the embarrassment . . . or we did mad dances. Then we got to hugging each other. Now we do the Buddhist bit . . . arms around. It's just saying hello, that's all." In his song "Help!" John had said that when he was younger, he'd never needed anybody's help in any way, but those days were gone and his sense of self-assurance and independence had vanished in the haze, and, as Cynthia realized, he now seemed to need his bandmates more than ever.

John was never afraid to expose and explore his own insecurities and vulnerabilities, but his weaknesses were almost always superseded by his adventurous and forward-looking spirit, and when six months earlier he had recklessly declared to the *Evening Standard*'s Maureen Cleave that the

Beatles were more popular than Jesus, he also told her: "We [the Beatles] can't go on holding hands forever. We have been Beatles as best as we ever will be—those four jolly lads. But we're not those people any more. We are old men. We can't go on hopping on *Top of the Pops* forever. . . . We can't develop the singing because none of us can sing in tune. We've got to find something else to do. Paul says it's like leaving school and finding a job. It's just like school, actually, because you have the group to lean on, and then suddenly find you're on your own. What we've got to do is find something we can put the same energy into as we did into being Beatles. And that's why I go around taping and writing and painting." And he would tell *Look* magazine's Leonard Gross that "I feel I want to be them all—painter, writer, actor, singer, player, musician. I want to try them all, and I'm lucky enough to be able to. I want to see which one turns me on." So when Richard Lester, director of *A Hard Day's Night* and *Help!*, offered John a role in an absurdist antiwar comedy film that he was about to direct called *How I Won the War,* John immediately accepted without even reading the script, and explained to Gross that "apart from wanting to do [this film] because of what it stands for, I want to see what I'll be like when I've done it."

John flew to Hanover, Germany, on September 5 to prepare for his role as Private Gripweed, a Cockney-accented orderly under the command of a British lieutenant called Ernest Goodbody, played by Michael Crawford, whose mission was to lead a squad of British "musketeers" to construct a cricket pitch behind enemy lines during the North African campaign of World War II.

But because John couldn't wear his Beatles hairstyle in a film set in the 1940s, he had agreed to undergo an altering of his facial appearance. A German barber performed the ritual shearing ceremony in the break-fast room of a hotel bar, first cutting off John's bangs, then trimming the back and sides, combing the front away from his forehead, and then shaving off his sideburns. According to Steve Turner, the discarded hair was incinerated despite an earlier plan to distribute it as prizes for a

A HARD DAY'S NIGHTS

competition run by the German teen magazine *Bravo*, although a four-inch lock of John's hair, squirreled away by the German barber, wound up on the auction block in 2016 and sold for thirty-five thousand US dollars. John was pleased with the haircutting rite of passage and said, "I've got a new face now."

But the transformation wasn't quite complete. John was required to wear glasses for the role of Gripweed, and he was fitted with circular, wire-rimmed Windsor glasses (often called "granny" glasses) with round lenses and a saddle bridge, and eyeglass temples that wrapped around his ears. John was extremely nearsighted, and as a teenager he had a pair of thick horn-rimmed eyeglasses that his hero Buddy Holly made famous, but those glasses didn't chime with John's then tough-rocker persona, and he refused to wear them in public, just as he refused to wear the British National Health Service's government-issued eyeglasses when he was young. Eventually he would take to wearing contact lenses, but when he first began performing, he used to tape the lyrics of a song on the back of his guitar and would squint at them if he forgot the words. There are many Mr. Magoo–type stories told about him, one of which describes John walking down the street, and upon hearing someone calling out his name from afar, he waved back, but it turned out that the recipient of his wave was a lamppost. The most uproarious of these stories, however, was recounted by Paul, who recalled that John once mistakenly thought that an outdoors Christmas nativity scene in Paul's Liverpool neighborhood was a family sitting in their backyard playing cards in the middle of the night!

The production of *How I Won the War* got underway in northern Germany on September 6, and a transformed John Lennon made an indelible first impression. "We expected someone a bit kinky, bitchy, arrogant," one actor told Leonard Gross, "but he's none of those things, he's completely natural," and another commented: "I don't think he does anything with a conscious thought of trying to impress. He's remarkably free, he doesn't act the part. . . . He's got a certain inborn, prenatal talent." But as John revealed to Gross: "I was just a bundle of nerves the first day.

I could hardly speak I was so nervous. My first speech was in a forest, on patrol. I was supposed to say, 'My heart's not in it anymore,' and it wasn't. I went home and said to myself, 'Either you're not going to be like that, or you're going to give up.' I don't mind talking to the camera—it's people that throw me." But he didn't give up. During the brief shoot in Germany John appeared in only two scenes, and after ten days the director, actors, and film crew traveled to Spain, where they spent the next six weeks completing the film in the Tabernas Desert, twenty miles north of the city of Almería, where John would live for the duration of the shoot.

During the 1960s the semiarid Tabernas Desert, with its sand dunes, prickly pear cacti, arroyos, tumbleweed, and dry winds blowing south from the surrounding mountains, served as a cinematic stand-in for the deserts in North Africa, Arabia, the southwestern United States, and northern Mexico, and was the location for film classics such as *Lawrence of Arabia, Exodus,* and Sergio Leone's spaghetti westerns *A Fistful of Dollars, For a Few Dollars More, The Good, the Bad, and the Ugly,* and *Once upon a Time in the West.* "It's like the moon, you know," John told the American journalist Fred Robbins, "just desert and sand and hills . . . not very nice to look at."

The city of Almería is on Spain's southeast Mediterranean coast, 340 miles south of Madrid, and when John arrived there on September 19 with his friend Neil Aspinall—the Beatles' roadie who was accompanying him during the film shoot—they first stayed in a small, cheerless hostel apartment called El Delfin Verde (the Green Dolphin) near El Zapillo beach. The role of Private Gripweed was a minor one—John appears on-screen for less than eight minutes—so he spent much of his spare time at the Green Dolphin. He had a nylon-stringed classical Spanish guitar, a portable cassette tape recorder, and some cassette tapes; one afternoon during siesta time he took the guitar out of its case, sat cross-legged on the bed, inserted a tape in the recorder, placed it next to him, pressed PLAY, and started strumming the strings. The twentieth-century Italian composer Giacinto Scelsi wrote: "A sound is the very first movement of the unmovable, and *that* is the beginning of creation." From the very first gentle, almost drone-like rhythmic pulsations in 4/4 time emerged the half-humming, half-murmuring sounds of some inchoate words—*There's no one on my wavelength / I mean it's either too high or too low / That is you can't, you know, tune in / But it's all right / That is I think it's not too bad*— and this was the beginning of the creation of what would turn out to be "Strawberry Fields Forever." John would later explain: "I was trying to describe how I felt, but I wasn't sure *how* I felt," and this new song was his attempt to find out.

He was about to celebrate his twenty-sixth birthday on October 9, but he was feeling uprooted and disconnected, and as he would later admit to *Playboy's* David Sheff: "It did me a lot of good to get away, but it *was* a withdrawal." To cheer himself up, he asked his English chauffeur, Les Anthony, to make the 1,400-mile drive to Almería in John's 1965 black Rolls-Royce Phantom V. The car had blacked-out windows, a fold-down bed, and was outfitted with a portable refrigerator, a telephone, a TV, a "floating" record player that absorbed road bumps, and external speakers from which John would blast out recordings of the "Colonel Bogey March"—featured in the film *The Bridge on the River Kwai*—Peter Sellers comedy sketches, and farmyard sound effects. (Startled residents nicknamed the vehicle "El Fúnebre," or "The Hearse.")

It was fun, and John enjoyed hanging out with his costar Michael Crawford, but complained: "I had a few laughs and games of Monopoly on the film, but it didn't work. I didn't meet anyone else I liked," so he decided to invite Cynthia, Ringo, and Maureen to visit him. But when they arrived in Almería—"I was never so glad to see the others. Seeing them made me feel normal again," he said—they immediately realized that they needed to find better and larger accommodations. While John was on the set, Cynthia and Maureen discovered and rented a mid-nineteenth-century, thirteen-bedroom villa called Santa Isabel on the outskirts of the city where film stars such as Peter O'Toole, Clint Eastwood, and Brigitte Bardot had previously stayed. "It'll take days just to explore this place,"

John commented upon seeing it for the first time, and in his memoir *Lifted* Ringo recalled: "You expect all kinds of heroes with swords to come swinging round the corner on a chandelier! What a great place for parties. I was convinced beyond all doubt the villa housed many beautiful spirits." But it was the spirit of another place that may have been the inspiration for the creation of John's new song.

It all began in 1945, when the then-five-year-old John began to live with his aunt Mimi Smith and her husband in a semidetached house called Mendips in the middle-class Liverpool suburb of Woolton. His father, Alf, was a merchant sailor who was continually away at sea, and during one of his absences his wife, Julia, had taken up with a wine steward named Bobby Dykins, who worked at a Liverpool Hotel and who had impregnated her. Realizing that she wasn't going to be able to continue to take full responsibility for her son, she gave custody of John to her sister Mimi. Alf went back to sea, but returned a year later with the intention of removing John from Mimi's home and taking him to New Zealand where he planned to emigrate, and he asked John to choose between him and his mother. Emotionally torn, John chose to stay with his mother, but Julia soon returned John to Mimi. Alf abandoned him, and John would years later tell Hunter Davies that he soon forgot his father, remarking: "It was like he was dead." Alf tried to get in touch with John only in 1964—he claimed that he didn't know who the Beatles were—when he was working as a kitchen porter at the Greyhound Hotel at Hampton Court in Middlesex and someone showed him a photo of John in a newspaper and asked if Alf was related to him. He immediately traveled down to London and went to the office of Brian Epstein and declared: "I'm John Lennon's father." John at first rejected his father's plea that "you can't turn your back on your family, no matter what they've done," but later relented and contacted Alf, telling Cynthia, "Alright, Cyn. He's a bit wacky, like me."

Julia never divorced Alf but lived with Dykins, with whom she had two daughters, as his common-law wife for the rest of her life. Julia was a vibrant and unconventional woman. Mimi, who was caring but strict and conventional, forbade John to have a record player and detested rock and roll music, but John would frequently visit Julia at her home, and she would play him Elvis Presley records and would dance around the kitchen with him while wearing a pair of knickers on her head. Julia played the banjo and the ukulele and taught John how to play those instruments, and when he was fifteen she bought him his first guitar—Mimi told him, "The guitar's all right for a hobby, John, but you'll never make a living at it." And after John met Paul, they would sometimes come by with their guitars, and Julia would take out her banjo and washboard and jam with the boys in her kitchen.

A five-minute walk from Mendips was a Salvation Army orphanage called Strawberry Field, a late nineteenth-century Gothic Revival mansion with red wrought iron gates and Gothic casements, and on its six acres were cypress trees, brambles, exotic plants, and an untamed, overgrown wooded garden. It was here that when John was young, he and his three rambunctious compatriots Nigel Walley, Ivan Vaughan, and Pete Shotton—they called themselves the Outlaws in homage to the little band of troublemakers in Richmal Crompton's subversive *Just William* children's books that John adored—would scale the sandstone wall, climb trees, make secret dens, reenact scenes from their favorite books and radio series, and play indefatigably to their heart's content, echoing the sentiments of William Blake's poem "Nurse's Song" ("No, no let us play, for it is yet day, / And we cannot go to sleep; / Besides, in the sky the little birds fly, / And the hills are all covered with sheep"). Mimi, like the poem's admonishing nurse ("Then come home, my children, the sun is gone down, / And the dews of night arise"), sternly advised John not to sneak onto the grounds, saying that it was private property, and John would reply, "They can't hang you for it," which he would later convert into the line "And nothing to get hung about" in "Strawberry Fields Forever." Every summer there was a fundraising summer fete on the orphanage grounds, with stalls selling cakes, cotton candy, and lemonade, and outdoor party games with prizes, and as Mimi told the biographer Albert Goldman, "He used to hear the Salvation Army band, and he would pull me along, saying, 'Hurry up, Mimi—we're going to be late!'"

In an interview I did with John for *Rolling Stone* magazine in 1968, he mentioned to me that "a part of 'Strawberry Fields' was written in a big Spanish house." In 1999 Javier Adolfo Iglesias, who was a journalist for the newspaper *La Voz de Almería* and a diehard Beatles and John Lennon fan, came across that interview and wondered what Spanish house John was referring to, so he undertook to find out. After weeks of investigation, he discovered a semiderelict mansion known locally as El Cortijo Romero, which had been abandoned for thirty years, and by rummaging around the entrance to the grounds he uncovered a name plaque hidden by weeds above the gatepost that read *Santa Isabel*. Iglesias had seen photographs of the Strawberry Field orphanage in Liverpool, and it suddenly struck him that the villa's wrought iron gate strikingly resembled the red wrought iron gate of Strawberry Field. He then walked around the property and later described what he saw: "There were the same elements as Strawberry Field: the wild garden, the high fence, and the shouts of children playing in the school next door."

In attempting to understand the abiding nature of memory and its sway on the creative imagination, and of the double vision of childhood lived and childhood recalled, the nineteenth-century Italian poet and philosopher Giacomo Leopardi wrote (in Ottavio Mark Casale's translation): "Most of the indefinite images and feelings we do experience after childhood are nothing other than a memory of childhood; they point back to it, they depend and derive from it; they are as it were an influx and consequence of it. . . . So that the present sensation does not come directly from things, is not an image of objects but [rather] of the childhood image: a remembrance, a repetition, an echoing or reflection of the old image." And like Iglesias, I think it's plausible that in John's

mind the memory of Strawberry Field re-echoed when he took up res-
idence in Santa Isabel and continued to develop the new song that he
had begun working on at the Green Dolphin and which he first titled
"It's Not Too Bad."

He recorded six takes of the song during the six weeks that he spent
in Almería—they have made the rounds on bootlegs and online sites for
many years—but they only began to take on a semblance of the completed song when John moved to Santa Isabel, where for the first time,
in takes 5 and 6, which he recorded in one of the Santa Isabel bathrooms
whose acoustics he preferred, he begins to sing about "going to Strawberry Fields." (John added the *s* to the word *field*.) It isn't certain that he
was then aware that the name of the orphanage derived from the rows of
strawberries that had originally grown in its once-lush gardens, but when
I interviewed him in 1968 he simply said, "But Strawberry Fields—I mean,
I have visions of *strawberry fields*."

"Strawberry Fields Forever" is a song of continuous self-discovery and
self-scanning—as the Spanish poet Antonio Machado wrote: "Walker,
there is no path, / You make the path as you walk"—and as John informed
me, "I was writing it in bits and bits and bits and I wanted the lyrics to be
the way you and I are talking now, like *talkingIjusthappentobesinging*—just
like that." In the process of creating the song you can hear him on these
work tapes continually hesitating, changing gears, reconsidering, reshap-
ing, revising—he would early on substitute the word *tree* for the word
wavelength in the song's second verse, which was the first track he worked
on—and, like a spider, he slowly secreted liquid words into what would
very gradually become solid verses. As Tim Riley perspicaciously writes
in his biography *Lennon: The Man, the Myth, the Music*: "The working
tapes show him going over and over his key phrases, repeating them as if
constantly questioning their resilience, and they survived many puzzled
exams. Yet no matter how often he returned to the work, its uncertainties
only deepened. . . . In one of the few examples of Lennon's songwriting
habits, it's almost as if he converses with the song daily to see how it

responds, if it suggests new words or melodic patterns as he nudges it forward. With his personal life a quandary, his songwriting provided a distinct yet tremulous answer."

The filming of *How I Won the War* wrapped on November 6, and John flew back to England the next day. In the two-week interim between his return from Spain and the Beatles' return to Abbey Road Studios on November 24, John worked assiduously in his music studio in the attic of his Kenwood mansion. He recorded nine unfettered multitracked home demos—now widely bootlegged—and experimented with "sound-on-sound" recording techniques in which he created overdubs by using two tape machines, playing back a demo that he had previously recorded on one tape machine and then overdubbing it with a new live guitar and vocal performance onto a second tape machine. He double-tracked his lead vocals onto other pre-recorded takes and played and overdubbed the sounds of his electric guitar, as well as a pipe organ, vibes, wine glasses, and Mellotron keyboard, the last of which Paul McCartney would use to create the opening melody for the recorded version of the song.

Throughout this demo recording process in his studio John was continuing to re-vision, flesh out, and complete the lyrics in a tortuous and roundabout way. The first work tapes that he recorded at the Green Dolphin had begun with nascent versions of the song's second verse ("No one I think is in my tree"), but when John moved to Santa Isabel, he created a partial version of the third verse ("Always, no sometimes, think it's me") and then a skeletal version of the chorus, which began "Let me take you down" and which he concluded with the line "Strawberry Fields and nothing." In his Kenwood demos, he finally wrote the song's first verse ("Living is easy with eyes closed"), changed "And nothing to get mad about" to "And nothing to get hung about," discarded "Strawberry Fields and nothing" as the chorus's concluding line, opting instead for "Strawberry Fields forever," and chose that line to be the new title for his song.

✣

The Beatles returned to Abbey Road Studios on November 24, 1966. It was the first time that their recording engineer, Geoff Emerick, had seen them since they had completed *Revolver* five months before, but as he would later say, "It might as well have been five years. They all looked so different." The clean-shaven, moptopped Fab Four were now looking more like what Lennon biographer Philip Norman described as Mexican revolutionaries. John, Paul, George, and Ringo sported horseshoe "Zapata" mustaches—John was now almost always wearing his post–Private Gripweed "granny" glasses—and George had a Vandyke beard. They had forsworn their touring days, removed their Beatles masks, and were now ready to expand on the technical achievements of *Revolver* and embark on their own version of a revolutionary recording journey of a thousand miles.

"Every time we went back into the studios," Ringo would later explain in *The Beatles Anthology,* "there was a period of wondering whose song we would start with. Nobody wanted to submit the first song because by then it was Lennon *or* McCartney more than Lennon *and* McCartney. So they'd say, 'What have you got?' . . . 'Well, what have *you* got?'" John had something to offer, and he took his acoustic guitar out of his case and, standing up, played them his new song. "When John sang 'Strawberry Fields' for the first time, just with an acoustic guitar accompaniment," George Martin recalled in his book *All You Need Is Ears,* "it was magic. It was absolutely lovely. I love John's voice anyway, and it was a great privilege listening to it," and in *Here, There, and Everywhere* Emerick wrote: "From the very first note it was obvious that this new Lennon song was a masterpiece. He had created a gentle, almost mystical tribute to some mysterious place, a place he called 'Strawberry Fields.' I had no idea what the lyric was about, but the words were compelling, like abstract poetry, and there was something magical in the spooky, detached timbre of John's voice. When he finished, there was a moment of stunned silence, broken by Paul, who in a quiet, respectful tone said simply, 'That is absolutely brilliant.'" George Harrison, too, felt something special was taking place. "I came back to England towards the end of October," he said in *The Beatles Anthology,* "and John got back from Spain. It was all predetermined when we'd meet again. Then we went in the studio and recorded 'Strawberry Fields.' I think at that point there was a more profound ambience to the band."

In *The Beatles Recording Sessions: The Official Abbey Road Studio Session Notes 1962–1970,* Mark Lewisohn states that "Strawberry Fields Forever" was among the most complicated and difficult Beatles songs to record. There were three distinct versions of the song, and it took twenty-six takes and about forty-five hours of studio time over a four-week period to complete. John had brought a demo tape of the song with him to the studio. It was an amalgam of his last two Kenwood demos, and on this final demo John sang the first line of the chorus as "Let me take you *back*"—this demo is included on *The Beatles Anthology 2* double-CD set released in 1996—and he changed it to *down* only when the Beatles began to record the first version of the song. John offered to play the demo for all of them, but they decided that they wanted to start recording immediately, and during the next seven and a half hours they began to construct the new song.

They first recorded a rhythm track, which consisted of John on rhythm guitar, George on slide guitar, Ringo on a snare drum and tom-toms, whose skins he had covered with tea towels to muffle the sounds, and Paul on the Mellotron, which John had brought down from Kenwood in its mahogany case for the sessions. The Mellotron was a keyboard that contained a bank of short, thirty-five magnetic audio tapes, and each key triggered a tape—not a tape loop—that was programmed to mimic other instruments such as flute, brass, and strings. They then overdubbed John's double-tracked lead vocal—he began this first recorded version of the song with its second verse ("Living is easy with eyes closed / Misunderstanding all you see")—and scat harmonies by John, Paul, and George. (An edited version of take 1 was also included in *The Beatles Anthology 2.*)

When the Beatles reconvened at the studio four days later, however, they decided to scrap the first version and began to work on what would

be a breakthrough second version. It opened with Paul's spectral Mellotron "flute" introduction after which you hear John for the first time beginning the song—at the inspired suggestion of Martin—with the chorus
("Let me take you down / 'Cos I'm going to Strawberry Fields"). John then
double-tracked his voice, and piano and bass overdubs were added, creating what became take 7. Three lengthy sessions were devoted to recording
this second version, and a rough mono mix was run off and acetates were
ordered so that the Beatles could listen to this version at home. But after
doing so, John told Martin the following day that he didn't find it satis-
factory. Martin asked him how he wanted the song arranged, and John
replied, "I don't know, I just think it should somehow be heavier." Martin
sounded him out as to what he specifically had in mind, but John just
repeated that he wanted it to be "just kind of, y'know . . . heavier." Martin
suggested that some outside musicians be brought in, and John liked the
idea and requested that Martin use "strings and a bit of brass," and added:
"Do a good job, George. Just make sure it's heavy."

Martin wrote an orchestral score for four trumpets and three cellos,
changing the key in order to allow the cellos to reach their bottom C note,
and then superimposed the instruments onto a backing track. Meanwhile,
while Martin and Emerick were out on the town one night attending the
premiere of Cliff Richard's film *Finders Keepers,* the maintenance engineer, Dave Harries, was playing the role of the Cat in the Hat in the studio
and decided to make his mark while the grown-ups were away with an
impromptu freak-out. As he informed Mark Lewisohn, "Soon after I had
lined up the microphones and instruments in the studio that night, ready
for the session, the Beatles arrived, hot to record. There was nobody else
there but me so I became producer/engineer. We recorded Ringo's cym-
bals, played them backwards, Paul and George were on timps [timpani]
and bongos, Mal Evans played tambourine, we overdubbed the guitars,
everything. It sounded great. When George and Geoff came back I scut-
tled upstairs because I shouldn't really have been recording them." But the
following day Martin decided to use parts of this wild sonic party—Martin

described it as "mayhem but great fun"—and overdubbed them with backward tape loops, plucked piano, and the sounds of a zither-like Indian instrument called the swarmandal that George Harrison had brought to the studio. "I'd just gotten back from India," George would explain, "and my heart was still out there. I was losing interest in being 'fab' at that point," and in the midst of this mayhem one can also faintly hear John mumbling the words "Calm down, Ringo" and "Cranberry sauce." (Beatles conspiracy theorists, who claimed that Paul had died in November and had been replaced in the Beatles by a doppelgänger, swore that what John had really intoned was "I buried Paul.")

The remake was now complete, and everything seemed to be locked in, but John had been spending hours listening to the acetates of the two versions of the song at home, and as Martin recalled: "John told me that he liked both versions of 'Strawberry Fields'—the original, lighter song and the intense, scored version—but he said to me 'Why don't you join the beginning of the first one to the end of the second one?' 'There are two things against it,' I replied. 'They are in different keys and different tempos. Apart from that, fine.' 'Well,' he said, 'you can fix it, George.'" George asked Emerick, "What do you think, Geoff?"

Today, a computer can easily change the pitch or tempo of recordings independently of each other, but in 1966 the only things Emerick and Martin had at their disposal were a pair of editing scissors, two tape machines, and a varispeed control. The problem was that as soon as you sped up a tape, the pitch went up, while slowing down a tape lowered the pitch. Fortunately, the two takes that John wanted spliced together—takes 7 and 26—were only a semitone apart, and the tempos were also fairly close, so by speeding up the playback of the first take and slowing down the playback of the second, Emerick was able to get them to match in both pitch and tempo. All he had to do was to find a suitable edit point at which to splice the two versions. The precise point he picked happened to fall exactly sixty seconds into the orchestral score's second chorus, on the word *going* ("Let me take you down / 'Cos I'm // *going* to . . ."). Now it was a matter of when to alter the playback speeds, and Martin and Emerick decided to allow the second half to play all the way through at the slower speed, and with a bit of practice, Emerick was able to gradually increase the speed of the first take, right up to the moment where he and Martin knew that they were going to do the edit. But since take 7 didn't include a chorus after the first verse, he also spliced in the first seven words of the second chorus from that take. Once the cut was made, however, the change was so subtle as to be virtually unnoticeable. It was a remarkable feat of technical legerdemain and prestidigitation.

On the evening of December 22, just three months after John had sat on his bed at the Green Dolphin in Almería and sang the lines "There's no one on my wavelength / I mean it's either too high or too low / That is you can't, you know, tune in / But it's all right / That is I think it's not too bad," Emerick and Martin were working late at Abbey Road Studios. Just a few minutes after completing the final edit, John happened to come by unannounced to see how things were progressing. He sat down, and they played him the transfigured version of "Strawberry Fields Forever." Emerick stood in front of the tape machine so that John couldn't see the splice go by, and a few seconds after it had, John asked if the deed had been done. 'Sure has,' Emerick replied. "Well, good on yer, Geoffrey!' John said, ecstatically. Emerick and Martin played the recording for John over and over again that night, and each time, according to Emerick, John would simply say "Brilliant. Just brilliant."

And now it was Paul's turn to shine.

Paul was fifteen and John was almost seventeen when he saw Paul standing there. It was July 6, 1957, an unusually hot summer's day, and John's skiffle / rock and roll band, the Quarrymen, was playing at the St. Peter's Church fete in Woolton. Ivan Vaughan, who was a member of John's Outlaws gang, was also a friend of Paul's and had asked him if he wanted to go to the fete. Paul himself was already a skillful guitarist and said sure, he wasn't doing anything. "I remember coming into the fete and seeing all the sideshows," Paul recounted to *Record Collector* magazine in 1995. "And also hearing all this great music wafting in from this little Tannoy [loud-speaker] system. It was John and the band. I remember I was amazed and thought, 'Oh great,' because I was obviously into the music. I remember John singing a song called 'Come Go with Me.' He'd heard it on the radio. He didn't really know the verses, but he knew the chorus. The rest he just made up himself. I just thought, 'Well, he looks good, he's singing well and he seems like a great lead singer to me.' Of course he had his glasses off, so he really looked suave," and Paul added: "I remember John was good. He was really the only outstanding member, all the rest kind of slipped away."

Paul and Ivan wandered around the fair afterward, and Ivan suggested that they go to the church's social hall, where the band was hanging out before playing its evening set, and Paul liked the idea. In fact, Paul had sported himself up for the fete. One of the hit songs that summer was "A White Sport Coat (And a Pink Carnation)," by the American country music star Marty Robbins, and Paul had followed suit and outfitted himself with a long-lapeled white sport coat, with sparkling metallic threads, that reached almost to his knees, and black drainpipe trousers. As soon as he got to the social hall, he straightaway picked up one of the Quarrymen's guitars and rotated it to play left-handed, and then launched into Eddie Cochran's "Twenty Flight Rock," a song with an adrenalized cascade of words—"So I walked one, two flight, three flight, four / Five, six, seven flight, eight flight more / Up on the twelfth I'm startin' to drag"—and everyone took notice: a left-handed guitarist playing a right-handed guitar. Paul also fooled around on a nearby piano, careening through Jerry Lee Lewis's "Whole Lotta Shakin' Goin' On," and he remembers John leaning over and "contributing a deft right hand in the upper octaves and surprising me with his beery breath."

John was amazed by the number of chords that Paul knew, as well as by his ability to remember the correct lyrics to the song, and as he told Hunter Davies: "I was very impressed by Paul playing 'Twenty Flight Rock.' I half thought to myself, 'He's as good as me.' I'd been kingpin up to then. Now, I thought, 'If I take him on, what will happen? . . . Was it better to have a guy who was better than the people I had in? To make the group stronger, or to let me be stronger? Instead of going for an individual thing we went for the strongest format—equals. I turned round to him right then on first meeting and said, 'Do you want to join the group?' And he said 'yes' the next day." Paul, however, recalls it differently, and stated that several days later Pete Shotton, who played washboard in the Quarrymen and who was another one of John's Outlaw comrades, met Paul by chance when they were out bicycling and said, 'Hey, Paul, it was good the other day, and we've been having a talk. Would you like to join the group?' Paul said he'd have to think about it, but he was thrilled by the offer and asked Ivan to tell John that he agreed to join the band.

A few months later, Paul introduced John to the then-fourteen-year-old George Harrison, a schoolmate with whom he occasionally played guitar and figured out chords together. (Hearing about a guitarist who knew the correct fingering for the B7 chord, Paul and George made a pilgrimage across town to find him.) Paul suggested to John that he consider George for the band, and his audition took place on the upper deck of a Liverpool double-decker bus. George took out his guitar and played the song "Raunchy"—a twangy guitar instrumental by Bill Justis—and it was so note-perfect that, in spite of George's age, John said, "Okay, you come in," but he did so trepidatiously, explaining in *The Beatles Anthology* that "George looked even younger than Paul, and Paul looked about ten with his baby face, but we asked George to join because he knew more chords." As John admitted to *Playboy*'s David Sheff, "I could only play the mouth organ and two chords on a guitar when I met Paul. I tuned the guitar like a banjo. I'd learned guitar from my mother who only knew how to play banjo, so my guitar only had five strings on it. Paul taught me how to play the guitar proper, but I had to learn the chords left-handed because Paul is left-handed. So I learned them upside down and I'd go home and reverse them. . . . Doesn't mean to say he has a greater talent, but his musical education was better."

Paul's father, Jim, who worked for most of his life in the cotton trade, was a trumpet player and pianist who had led Jim Mac's Jazz Band in the 1920s and played in ragtime and jazz bands in Liverpool and took Paul to brass-band concerts. There was an upright piano in the living room, and he urged Paul to take piano lessons, but Paul preferred to learn by ear. For his fourteenth birthday he received a nickel-plated trumpet from his father, and Paul played it for a short time, but he wanted to be able to sing songs, and as he said, "it became clear to me fairly quickly that you couldn't sing with a trumpet stuck in your mouth." So with Jim's permission he traded the trumpet in for a Zenith Model 17 acoustic guitar, but when he brought it home, he couldn't figure out how to play it. He didn't realize that it was because he was left-handed, and it wasn't until he saw Slim Whitman [the American country music singer], who was also left-handed, on television that he understood he was holding the guitar the wrong-way round. So he restrung the guitar "upside-down," mounted a little pickup near the bridge, and he would use that guitar until the Beatles went to Hamburg.

Shortly after Paul's mother, Mary, who was a nurse and midwife, died in October 1956, Paul wrote his first song, "I Lost My Little Girl," in which he describes waking up late one morning with his head in a whirl and understanding that he had lost his "little girl." (As he told the New Yorker's David Remnick, "You wouldn't have to be Sigmund Freud to recognize that the song is a very direct response to the death of my mother.") He then played it for John, and they decided to see if they could write as a team. They would sometimes skip school and get together whenever they could in the McCartneys' small terraced council house on Forthlin Road in the afternoon when Jim was at work (Paul and his brother, Mike, had their own keys to the house) and create their songs in the parlor. At that time, John had a guitar that was bought from the want ads, and Paul's guitar was also hardly of stellar quality. And because Paul was left-handed and John was right-handed, when they sat opposite each other with their guitars, they would be mirror images. Years later in his 1980 *Playboy* interview, John would describe their modus operandi: "Paul hits this chord, and I turn to him and say 'That's it! Do that again!' In those days we really used to write like that—both playing into each other's noses." They would trade words, swap suggestions, and place a tattered school exercise book on the floor. Paul would write down the words and chord sequences they came up with, and on the top of the first page he wrote "A Lennon–McCartney Original," and on each following page, "Another Lennon–McCartney Original."

Paul would later give an example of how they worked together. He had come up with the idea for "I Saw Her Standing There" and wrote the opening verse, rhyming "She was just seventeen" with "She'd never been a beauty queen." When John winced, Paul agreed that it was kind of corny, and they then searched for another rhyme for "seventeen"—"clean," "lean," "mean"—and thought of "She wasn't mean, you know what I mean," and finally the second line metamorphosed into "You know what I mean." "We inspire each other," John told the Irish journalist and musician BP Fallon in 1969. "We write how we write because of each other. Paul was there for five or ten years, and I wouldn't write like I write now if it weren't for Paul, and he wouldn't write like he does if it weren't for me." And even when they began to write more frequently on their own, they would still contribute lines and images to each other's songs.

John and Paul had toyed with the notion of writing songs about Liverpool for several years, and they had even thought of creating a stage musical about the city. In October 1965 John began writing lyrics to what was to become "In My Life," which he said was the first song he wrote that was consciously about his life, whose preliminary but ultimately discarded stream-of-consciousness lyrics depict a meandering, memory-laden ride on the number 5 bus into town from his home on Menlove Avenue, then up Church Road to the clock tower and down to the docks. He also had the line "Penny Lane is one I'm missing"—and perhaps he meant "missing" in both senses of that word. Paul took up where John left off. In an interview he gave to *Flip* magazine in December 1965 he said, "I like some of the things The Animals try to do, like the song Eric Burdon wrote about places in Newcastle on the flip of one of their hits. I still want to write a song about the places in Liverpool where I was brought up. Places like the Docker's Umbrella, which is a long tunnel through which the dockers go to work on Merseyside, and Penny Lane near my old home."

Penny Lane is a street in the south Liverpool suburb of Mossley Hill, but its name also refers to the area surrounding its junction with Allerton Road (and its bustling shopping area), Smithdown Road, and Smithdown Place, which was the location of a major bus terminus and transportation hub and which included a bus shelter located on its own "island"—"the shelter in the middle of a roundabout"—and which was where John and Paul would change buses when they wanted to visit each other and where they would often hang out together.

Penny Lane had a profound association for John. Before he moved to his aunt Mimi's house in Woolton when he was five years old, he lived with his mother and father, who was for most of the time away at sea, in his maternal grandparents' red-brick, three-bedroom house on nearby Newcastle Road. Paul had been a choirboy at St. Barnabas Church opposite the roundabout, but his most significant memories of Penny Lane were those from his early teenage years. The painter Jack B. Yeats—the brother of the poet William Butler Yeats—once said, "No one creates . . . the artist assembles memories," and Paul's memories of Penny Lane were reawakened in early December while the recording of "Strawberry Fields Forever" was taking place. The song struck a chord in him, so he decided to respond to it, and throughout that month he spent as much time as he could in the music room at the top floor of his three-story Edwardian house at 7 Cavendish Avenue in St. John's Wood, not far from

Abbey Road Studios, sitting at what he referred to as his "magic" Alfred E. Knight upright piano, which had recently been painted with psychedelic rainbow patterns by the painter David Vaughan. In Latin, the word *memoria* designates both "memory" and "imagination," and in "Penny Lane" Paul demonstrated that one could in fact create and imagine as well as assemble memories.

In "Penny Lane," he tells us, "there is a barber showing photographs / Of every head he's had the pleasure to know." There was in fact a real barbershop called Bioletti's, but it was located on Smithdown Place, which is at the end of Penny Lane, and it played a fascinating role in Beatles history, for it was here that John had had his baby curls cut when he was five, and it was where both Paul and George got their haircuts when they were teenagers. In the mid-1950s James Bioletti, the owner of the shop, was assisted by his eighty-year-old father, whom someone once described as "an octogenarian Edward Scissorhands with the shakes" and whose stylistic repertoire, like his son's, mainly consisted of "a short back and sides." But Bioletti had recently made a new hire, a young Greek barber named Andre, who specialized in "Tony Curtis" and "Jeff Chandler" cuts. Liverpool teenagers prayed that they might find their heads in his hands, and the shop window proudly displayed head shots of some of those fortunate teenage customers' "cuts."

On the same block as the barbershop was a bank, and for the occasion Paul envisioned a banker with a motorcar who never wears a mac even in the pouring rain while little children laugh at him behind his back. There was also a fire station in the Penny Lane neighborhood, but it was about a half mile down the road on Mather Avenue, and, with an inspired image assist from John, Paul introduces us to "a fireman with an hourglass / And in his pocket is a portrait of the Queen," and then adds: "He likes to keep his fire engine clean / It's a clean machine," two lines of which Paul was especially proud. ("You occasionally hit a lucky little phrase," he once said, "and it becomes more than a phrase.") And when Paul tells us that behind the Penny Lane bus shelter in the middle of the roundabout "a pretty nurse is selling poppies from a tray," he drew on his memory of Remembrance Day, which takes place every November 11 in Great Britain when people buy artificial poppies, usually sold by former and serving members of the armed forces, to pay tribute to the soldiers who died in the trenches of World War I. But he dreamed up the pretty nurse, and in the process created one of his luckiest and most inspired lines: "And though she feels as if she's in a play / She is anyway."

In breaks during the recording of John's song, Paul had been religiously listening to the Beach Boys' album *Pet Sounds,* which had been released in May 1966, on a portable record player that he'd brought to the studio. "It blew me out of the water," he said, and he was particularly transfixed by the song "God Only Knows," which he praised as "the classic of the century," "the greatest song ever written," and, as he told BBC Radio 1 in 2007, "one of the few songs that reduces me to tears every time I hear it." Even John admitted that when the song came out the "world perked up." It was a mutual admiration society. Brian Wilson was himself a Beatles enthusiast who said that *Rubber Soul* was one of *his* favorite albums of all time, and he confessed to *Reverb* magazine that "I listened to *Rubber Soul,* smoked some marijuana, and was so blown away that I went right over to my piano and wrote 'God Only Knows' with a friend of mine [Tony Asher]." (A personal note: To me, the most beautiful song on *Pet Sounds* is "Don't Talk (Put Your Head on My Shoulder)"—certainly another one of the greatest songs ever written!)

On the evening of December 29, the Beatles arrived at Abbey Road Studios to begin the process of creating "Penny Lane," one that would take three weeks to accomplish. But this was Paul's moment, and Geoff Emerick was convinced that the best way to obtain the "really clean American sound" that Paul desired was to record each instrument on its own in order to eliminate any leakage or "bleed" (a sound picked up by a microphone from an unintended source), and Paul agreed. Ordinarily, recording sessions would start with the Beatles laying down a basic rhythmic track and then adding overdubbed instruments. In this case, however, Paul took over the session and said that he wanted to begin by recording the first of what would turn out to be a series of overdubbed piano parts. The first piano part, which went onto track 1 of the four-track tape, consisted of a constant pulse of staccato chords; then, as the three other Beatles sitting at the back of the studio watched him layering multiple keyboard parts, Paul created a second one, played this time through a Vox guitar amplifier with vibrato and reverb, which went onto track 2. Track 3 had another piano part, which Paul performed on what was known as the "Mrs Mills Piano"—it got its name from an English recording artist from the 1960s named Mrs. Gladys Mills—a slightly detuned Steinway Vertegrand upright that produced a playful honky-tonk sound. Ringo also added some jangly tambourine sounds. And then on track 4 Paul played both the piano and the harmonium, drawing from it some high-pitched whistles, fed once again through a Vox guitar amplifier, and then superimposed on them rat-a-tat-tat percussion effects and sustained cymbal notes. For Paul, it had been a hard day's night's work.

When the Beatles returned to the studio the following evening, nothing could be done until Emerick reduced the previous day's now-filled four tracks onto track 1 of a new tape, thereby freeing up three tracks for more recording and overdubs. But because that took until after midnight, the only thing they had time to record was Paul's lead vocal, backed by John. When they finished, it was 3 a.m., so the other overdubs intended for the song had to be put off until the new year.

On January 4 and then January 6, things began to progress more quickly. Overdubbed onto the tape were Paul playing bass guitar—his bass line provided the powerful underpinning to the song—George lead guitar, John on rhythm, and Ringo on drums. Since all four tracks were once again filled, another reduction mix was made, and then John and George Martin contributed some additional piano parts, John played conga drums, and John, Paul, and George did scat singing. Emerick reports that Ringo paid a visit to the studio's legendary sound effects cupboard, which was under the stairs in Studio Two—a repository of whistles, hooters, thunder machines, chains, and a cash register that the Beatles had ransacked for their recording of "Yellow Submarine"—and uncovered a fireman's hand-bell, and Ringo's clanging of the bell was overdubbed whenever Paul sang about the Penny Lane fireman with his "clean machine." Years later Paul demonstrated with video footage from the 1990s that it was actually a set of tubular bells that Ringo had used, but as one of the characters in the film *The Man Who Shot Liberty Valance* famously remarked: "When the legend becomes fact, print the legend."

Before the Beatles took off for the weekend, Paul asked Martin if he could bring in some outside classical musicians and write a score for a bevy of instruments, including trumpets, flutes, oboes, a flügelhorn, and a bowed double bass. Martin did so, and the resulting music was over-dubbed on both January 9 and 12. Combined with Paul's bass playing and backing vocals from John and George, this track seemed to Emerick to be close to completion. But on the evening of January 11, Paul had been watching a late-night BBC television program that featured a live per-formance of Bach's *Brandenburg Concerto No. 2,* and he saw and heard a trumpeter playing a glittering virtuoso solo, which, in the opinion of the renowned English trumpeter David Blackadder, who specializes in baroque music, is "perhaps the greatest test of stamina in the entire clas-sical repertoire for a trumpet player." It was an epiphanic moment for Paul, and in a flash he came up with an idea for what he felt would be the pièce de résistance for "Penny Lane."

The next morning an elated Paul told Martin about that dazzling per-formance and asked him what kind of tiny trumpet the musician was playing. Martin told him it was a piccolo trumpet and that the forty-year-old trumpeter was a friend of his named David Mason, who was at that time the principal trumpeter for the New Philharmonia Orchestra. Paul asked Martin if he could bring him into the studio and have him overdub a solo. On January 17 Mason arrived with nine trumpets, and Martin chose the B-flat piccolo trumpet, pitched an octave higher than the standard trumpet, for the recording, but there was no music prepared for him. As Mason described the scene in *The Beatles—an Oral History*: "Paul sat at the piano, played his few chords, and sang a bit, then went, *'Dum da digga dum.'* He said, 'Can you do that?' Then I did it and he said, 'No, up a bit. Yes, that's better. That sounds nice. Yes we'll keep that bit.' Then George Martin wrote it down." The solo took three hours to compose and just ten minutes to record, and as Mason told Mark Lewisohn, "They were jolly high notes, quite taxing. . . . Although Paul seemed to be in charge, and I was the only one playing, the other three Beatles were there too. They all had funny clothes on, candy-striped trousers, floppy yellow bow ties, etc. I asked Paul if they'd been filming because it really looked like they had just come off a film set. John Lennon interjected, 'Oh no mate, we always dress like this!'"

In *All You Need Is Ears,* Martin states that Mason's tour de force performance, which required meticulous breath and lip control, was note- and pitch-perfect. Paul, who was sitting next to Martin in the control room, spoke to Mason on the talkback mic and said how much he liked his performance but wondered if he could try it one more time. Mason told him that he couldn't play it any better, and Martin said to Paul, "Good God, you can't possibly ask the man to do that again . . . it's fantastic!" Paul finally acceded to his producer's assessment and mitigated the awkward situation by saying to Mason, "Okay, thank you, David. You're free to go now, released on your own recognizance."

The session was over, and the songs "Penny Lane" and "Strawberry Fields Forever" were released as a double A-side single in the United States on February 13, 1967, and in the United Kingdom four days later. The songs, however, were originally meant to be included on the Beatles' forthcoming *Sgt. Pepper's Lonely Hearts Club Band,* for which they had already recorded "When I'm Sixty-Four." But EMI Records wanted another Beatles single as soon as possible, and Brian Epstein (a managerial adherent of the out of sight, out of mind school of thought) was worried that the band's low public profile would diminish its popularity, and he asked Martin: "What have you got?" Martin said that he had two great songs and that "we could put them together and make a smashing single." He would later regret his decision for commercial reasons, and in his book *All You Need Is Ears,* he stated that "it was the biggest mistake in my professional life . . . If I had stopped to think for more than about a second, I would have realized that one great title would fight another." On the British record charts, the two double A-side songs were in fact counted separately so that one side canceled out the success of the other, and this broke the string of the Beatles' twelve consecutive number one hits, losing out to Engelbert Humperdinck's "Release Me."

Martin, and the Beatles themselves, also felt that when they released a single for the UK market, those two songs shouldn't be included on an album so as not to make the fans pay for those songs again—in America, Capitol Records, the sister company of EMI, didn't always follow this protocol—but an exception to this rule was when "Eleanor Rigby" and "Yellow Submarine" were released in the UK on the same day as *Revolver.* Over the years, a number of critics and many Beatles fans—both American and British—have maintained that "Strawberry Fields Forever" and "Penny Lane" rightly belonged on *Sgt. Pepper's Lonely Hearts Club Band,* and they have envisaged where those songs should have been placed on the album or, conversely, have debated what should have been eliminated from it in order to make room for those two songs.

But if their release as a single was a "mistake," it was a felix culpa—a happy fault—because to me and many others, this double A-side record is incontrovertibly a self-contained masterpiece, and the critical acclaim for it was and remains unparalleled. On its release, *Time* magazine praised it as "the latest example of the Beatles' astonishing inventiveness" and commented that "[they] have developed into the single most creative force in pop music. Wherever they go, the pack follows. And where they have gone in recent months, not even their most ardent supporters would ever have dreamed of. They have bridged the heretofore impassable gap between rock and classical, mixing elements of Bach, Oriental, and electronic music with vintage twang to achieve the most compellingly original sounds ever heard in pop music." In *The Beatles Diary* the British author and critic Peter Doggett described it as "the greatest pop record ever made" and "a record that never dates because it lives outside time." The *New Yorker*'s Adam Gopnik wrote that "with my chin only slightly out and leading, I'd even argue that this simple single was the most significant work of art produced in the 1960s, the one that articulated the era's hopes for a crossover of pop art and high intricacy." And George Martin stated unequivocally: "In my estimation, this was the best record we ever made."

The Beatles

My *Penny Lane* and *Strawberry Fields Forever*: the double A-side 45 rpm record I bought in Berkeley, California, on February 13, 1967.

All the People That Come and Go

FIVE CONVERSATIONS

BILL FRISELL

What we play is life.
—Louis Armstrong

The *New York Times* once described Bill Frisell as "the most significant and widely imitated guitarist to emerge in jazz since the beginning of the 1980s." Praised by Paul Simon, Elvis Costello, Justin Vernon, and Lucinda Williams ("My favorite guitarist in the whole world"), he has been called "the maestro of all guitar possibilities" by the British poet Michael Horovitz. As Philip Watson points out in his superb five-hundred-page biography—*Bill Frisell, Beautiful Dreamer: The Guitarist Who Changed the Sound of American Music*—Frisell's mastery of musical genres and forms ranges from "bluegrass to pop, Americana to avant-garde, blues to West African, folk to film music, ambient to alt-rock, country to classical." Frisell himself has said, "I'm just trying not to shut anything out."

I had dreamed of interviewing Bill Frisell after listening to his 2011 album *All We Are Saying . . .*, which comprises sixteen songs written by John Lennon both as a member of the Beatles and as a solo artist, as interpreted by Frisell and the violinist Jenny Scheinman, the pedal steel and acoustic guitarist Greg Leisz, the bassist Tony Scherr, and the drummer Kenny Wollesen. As Frisell once confessed, "I don't even know if I'd be playing guitar if it wasn't for the Beatles and John Lennon. This music—it's such a deep and important part of my life, it's in my blood. . . .

The music is so rich that I could just keep playing and playing it, it just keeps revealing more and more. . . . There's always something else going on there, it's the next step into the unexplainable."

I had been told that when Frisell was twelve years old, he had seen the Beatles perform on television on the legendary February 9, 1964, broadcast of *The Ed Sullivan Show,* and that it had been an epiphanic moment in his life. I wanted to ask him about that moment, as well as about "Strawberry Fields Forever" and "Penny Lane," and about his extraordinary fifty-year career. So I was overjoyed when in April 2022 he invited me to visit him at his home in Brooklyn. We spoke for several hours that day and continued our conversation two months later.

In "Love Minus Zero / No Limit" Bob Dylan sings: "My love she speaks like silence, / Without ideals or violence," and in *Thus Spake Zarathustra* Friedrich Nietzsche says: "The voice of beauty speaks softly." Bill Frisell is a soft-spoken person, and one listens to his silences as much as to his words, just as one listens to the silences as well as to the notes when he plays his guitar. It is beautiful to listen to them all.

"I read somewhere that the Beatles changed your life when you were twelve years old," I said to Bill as we sat down in his living room to begin our conversation.

"They did, totally," he responded.

I mentioned to him that the composer Steve Reich once revealed that his own life had suddenly changed when at the age of fourteen he heard Igor Stravinsky's *The Rite of Spring* for the first time. Reich said that he'd never previously heard any music before 1750 or after Wagner, nor any jazz. Then one day a friend came over to his house and said, "I've got something you've *really* got to hear," and they went to his friend's house and put on a recording of *The Rite of Spring.* "I remember looking outside," Reich recalled, "and it was like 'Is such a thing possible?' Suddenly, the universe opened up. It was like being in a house and someone says, 'There's one room you *haven't* seen.'"

"That's a perfect description of what happened when I first saw the Beatles on *The Ed Sullivan Show*," Bill told me.

"It was like a room you hadn't seen before?"

"But it wasn't a room," he explained, "it was *everything*. What was getting me wasn't so much the words but that *sound*, it was the sound of them together—but it's even bigger than that. It's just that thing about not having heard something like that before. Like I try to imagine what it would be like if it was 1927 and you walked into a bar and Louis Armstrong was playing. What would that sound like if you'd never heard it before? I guess I was lucky because I got to have that experience with the Beatles, but maybe it wasn't special to me because it happened to a lot of other people too."

"About seventy-three million people watched that show," I said.

"Yes, and I actually remember the day before and the day after, and all the kids in school were different the next day."

"So, it was like B.B.—Before Beatles—and A.B.—After Beatles?"

"It was something like that," Bill said, laughing. "Before then I had mostly been listening to the Beach Boys and surf music—the Ventures, the Astronauts—and groups like the Four Seasons. Peter, Paul and Mary. *American Bandstand* and Steve and Eydie on TV. That kind of stuff. But right after I saw the Beatles I got a paper route, and in the summer of 1965 I finally had enough money to buy my first electric guitar—a Fender Mustang—and then a friend of mine got a guitar, and the guy across the street got drums, and we started playing tunes by the Beatles, the Rolling Stones, and the Byrds.

"There was all this chaos in those days with the Vietnam War, but I really had a feeling that we were moving up out of it, that we were figuring it out. So much happened in 1964—the Civil Rights Act, Nelson Mandela was sentenced to life in prison, and I saw Martin Luther King, who won a Nobel Peace Prize that year, speak at a church. The school I went to was

racially and economically mixed—it was right in the middle of Denver—
and I was also playing clarinet, which was my first instrument, in bands
with Black kids. There was suffering all around, but I thought that if
people wanted to play music together, you had to figure out how to play
music, and that's like a blueprint for how people can actually function
together. Some people think it sounds like a joke, but I believe if everybody played a guitar, we might not have total peace on earth, but I don't
see how you could possibly have all of this terrible stuff going on. As you
work on music, there's tension and release and conflict and resolution,
and you realize that you're all in the same boat and that you are in this
and doing this together."

"It's like living all together on a yellow submarine," I said.

"[*Laughing*] Yes, and when you're playing with other people something special can happen—although it doesn't happen with everybody—
but when I'm playing a melody with someone else and we're playing
in unison, it's as if both instruments become one another, and I can't
tell who is who. It's a physical sensation. But the moment you begin to
wonder 'Is that him or me? Or her or me?'—as soon as you become aware
of that, it all goes away.

"Some years ago my daughter was working at an arts center in northern Vermont, and I was touring but had two days off, so I went to visit
her—I hadn't seen her for a while and we got to hang out. There was a
Ping-Pong table in the back of one of the rooms, and after dinner we
decided to play Ping-Pong. At first we started keeping score, but then I
said, Let's not keep score, let's just play, let's just see if we make it to 100
without messing up, and we're like hitting the ball back and forth, and
I'm getting really tired, my arms are getting tired, but we finally got to
100 . . . and we kept going, we were just in this zone, and we got to 608,
and right then in my mind I had the thought, I bet we can make it to 1,000
[*laughing*], but as soon as I had that thought, I missed it, it was over."

"This reminds me," I said, "of a centipede that starts thinking of how
many legs it has and then starts stepping all over itself. Or like Wile E.

Coyote running off a cliff and accelerating until he suddenly looks down, and down he goes."

"That's it. Totally," Bill agreed, laughing. "It's like when Sonny Rollins said that you can't think when you're playing because the music is happening too fast. And in music I'm always hoping to get to that place where you're just *in* it. You're playing with some other musicians, and you get that thing going, whether it's playing the same note or everyone's just playing together. But it also can happen when everyone is playing something different and you don't know if *you're* playing that or if *he* or *she* played it. When you get that *sound* and you don't know what it is anymore, you're just in this zone, and there's ecstasy in it. But as soon as you become aware of it, you lose it. And by the way, that's what I was hearing and feeling when I first saw the Beatles singing together on *The Ed Sullivan Show,* and that was one of the things that made me want to try to do that."

"The Spanish poet Antonio Machado," I said, "wrote a tiny poem which goes: 'To engage in a dialogue / First: ask a question / Then: listen.'"

"And that's the number one rule for playing music," Bill said. "Anything musical has a question in it. A note is a question—sometimes a phrase can be a question too—and then you listen to it and you consider it and then you have to find the answer. But it's also a statement, and then you get asked, Well, what did you mean? And you listen and respond, and then there are all these choices—play one note, but then what if you played a different note? This is true when I'm playing with other musicians, although it's the same when I play alone. But when you're with other musicians, you can be subversive, you can mess with it [*laughing*], you can be violent but nobody gets hurt.

"When I played clarinet in my high school band, my best friend, who also played the clarinet, used to sit next to me, and we would turn our clarinets upside down and play the music backward. We were being juvenile delinquent, smart-aleck jerks, but there's something to be said for that, because that's a way of learning how to be creative with the music.

"I recently saw Peter Jackson's *Get Back* Beatles documentary and noticed the way those songs would emerge from that kind of goofing off. It was amazing to see that process of going through what seems like chaotic goofing around, but that gets you in touch with yourselves. When I first saw the Beatles on TV, I couldn't pick out the individual people, but when I watched the documentary, just as a guitar player, what flipped me out was when George was playing something, and John and Paul were sort of out of tune, and I'm thinking that it was kind of messed up, but then suddenly they're all together. It had nothing to do with being in tune the way we talk about it in school. What the Beatles were doing all came from individual elements, but they just melded it all together. When you saw them working on their music, they were taking chances, and there's no way that would have happened if they just kind of wrote the song, and it had to go a certain way—you do this and I'll do that. For all the talk about all of the tension and about how the band was about to break up, what I was seeing was this incredible respect they had for each other."

"You saw *The Ed Sullivan Show* on February 9, 1964," I reminded Bill, "and just three years later, on February 13, 1967, the Beatles released a double A-side 45 rpm single comprising 'Strawberry Fields Forever' and 'Penny Lane,' and since I'm writing a book about those two songs I wanted to discuss them with you."

"I knew that we were going to be talking about them," Bill said, "so this morning I listened to them with headphones on. I've heard them a lot of times before, but this morning it was like, Oh my God, what's going on? They're so awesome and amazing and inspiring. It was like being a little kid and you're in that state when you're hearing and seeing something for the first time and it blows your mind, and I was really struck this time by the psychedelic sonic quality of both of the songs and by the texturally extraordinary orchestration. The Beatles and their producer George Martin were pushing things way past the limited production techniques available to them—they had to get everything on four tracks—but it was the Beatles' imaginations that did it. There were no limits on it.

Everybody's concerned about the materials that you're using—what kind of guitar, what kind of amp, what kind of pedals—but what's in our minds is so much more powerful.

"Every time I listen to these songs there's something I've never noticed before. You go *back* to them, but there's always something else to uncover, something more gets peeled away. Every one of those notes and chords contains a whole harmonic series, like a rainbow—it just goes on forever, above it and below it, and it's as if you can get inside it. They're so perfect, so powerful, and the recording stops time, it captures that moment when the songs were recorded. But I don't think those songs are finished yet, no matter how perfect that moment was, there's still more to discover in them. They're not dead yet."

"There's a poem by Emily Dickinson," I told Bill, "that goes: 'A word is dead / When it is said, / Some say. / I say it just / Begins to live / That day.'"

"And it makes total sense when you're talking about those songs, but it's also true about music in general, and it's the same when you're playing music. No matter how fully you realize whatever it is you're striving for, it just never ends. No matter how far you go, there's no way for you to finish it, you can never get it completely right. There's always something extraordinarily beautiful through that door and you want to check it out. Your imagination wants to go further than it's ever been, and you want to be in a place where you've never been before. And when you get there, the same thing happens again. It just doesn't stop, each note of the melody or each chord opens up all kinds of new worlds. You can't *finish* music, and all the greatest musicians I know of would be the first to tell you that. Anybody who says they've figured it all out probably hasn't. I could play a song like 'Strawberry Fields Forever' for the rest of my life and it will always be alive."

"I wonder if you could say something about the melodic and harmonic aspects of both 'Strawberry Fields Forever' and 'Penny Lane' and what kinds of worlds they open up."

"These two songs are crystallized and distilled," Bill explained. "They're not long but they're epic, and there's so much there."

[Bill picks up an acoustic guitar and occasionally plays some of the melodic lines and harmonies from the two songs as he talks about them.]

"'Penny Lane' is so beautifully rich texturally," Bill told me, "but it mostly stays in the same world for the entire song, whereas 'Strawberry Fields' is like, whoa, where are we going, we're suddenly thrown into these different worlds. I play the song in A, although you could play the entire thing in B-flat, but I think that that ambiguity exists because of the Mellotron introduction to the song, so the tuning got thrown off by that. And then when they added the brass and cellos, it got thrown off even more. And it also has these very odd rhythmic things—odd phrasings— but we've heard them so often that they sound natural. There's a 2/4 bar, then a 3/4 bar, then an extra bar—it's like Blind Willie Johnson. [Bill plays some examples of these phrasings.] The words determine the length of the phrases, so it breaks out of an even eight-bar pattern. It's as if the melody is asking the question, and then there's an answer to it, and then there are these incredible and unusual chords, similar to what Bill Evans played on the piano."

"And how does this differ from 'Penny Lane'?" I asked.

"Unlike 'Strawberry Fields,'" he said, "'Penny Lane' stays within a common symmetrical structure. And unlike John, there's more reference in Paul's work to the melodies and harmonies of earlier Tin Pan Alley songs, he had that language in his blood. But there are some weird harmonies in 'Penny Lane' as well."

[Bill takes up his guitar and plays the melody and harmonies of the lines "On the corner is a banker with a motorcar / And little children laugh at him behind his back."]

"That's all normal," Bill said. "But the lines [he now plays the melody and harmonies for "And the banker never wears a mac in the pouring rain / Very strange"] are super-advanced, Wayne Shorter–type harmonies. And the song modulates in an unusual way—the chorus ["Penny Lane is in my ears and in my eyes / There beneath the blue suburban skies"] modulates a whole step down but gives you the impression that it's lifting up. It's definitely not a normal modulation to go a whole step lower. And then when it goes back to the verse, there's a chord that would normally lead you into a minor chord but it instead goes back to a major chord. [Bill plays the chord.] It keeps circling around in that way."

"When Paul sings the words 'Meanwhile back,'" I observed, "the chords sound a little strange."

"And that's where it goes off," he replied. "That's the pivot chord. [Bill plays "Meanwhile back."] And then it modulates back to where it was, and that's the same place where the trumpet plays later on. And the very last time Paul sings the chorus again, instead of modulating back to A, he modulates the chorus up, and then it just ends. It's a beautiful technical structure.

"I feel funny saying this, but when I was in high school in Denver, I found an incredible guitar teacher named Dale Bruning—it was a miracle I found him. This was when I started getting more into jazz, and I probably wouldn't be playing if I hadn't met him. He had moved to Denver from Philadelphia, he knew Coltrane, and he was sort of an oasis of knowledge out there, and he turned me on to jazz music that I wanted to find out about, like Dizzy Gillespie and Oscar Peterson and Sonny Rollins. And the first time I heard Wes Montgomery I was blown away.

"So as I was finding out about this more complex music, I developed an attitude about what I'd been listening to before. And when Dale made some comment about how the Beatles' chord structures were incorrect or wrong, like they didn't move in a proper manner, for a moment there I thought that the Beatles might be naive and stupid music. But I eventually shook that off, and now, holy shit, with regard to musical forms and musical structures, songs like 'Strawberry Fields' and 'Penny Lane' are totally super high-level, sophisticated, and amazing."

"The poet William Blake," I mentioned, "once wrote: 'Improvement makes strait roads, but the crooked roads without Improvement are roads of Genius.'"

"Yes, that's the stuff that really makes me excited, and when I think of all of my heroes, they all went on the crooked roads. The Beatles too would try anything, and they were open to the possibility of making mistakes, and if your imagination is open, some of the most beautiful things come from those mistakes."

"John Lennon," I said, "once described how when the Beatles were working in the studio on his song 'Rain,' he took the tape of what they'd recorded that day back to his home so that he could listen to what they'd done. He put his headphones on and mistakenly placed the tape in the tape machine the wrong way round so that his vocal line came out sounding *backward*. John said that it blew his mind—'I was in a trance in the headphones,' he said—and wanted the entire song to be recorded backward, although they wound up just tagging it on as the song's coda, and it's said that this was the first time that reversed sounds appeared in a pop song. Miles Davis once remarked, 'Do not fear mistakes. There are none.' Do you agree?"

"Totally. There's a story about how when Herbie Hancock was playing with Miles, he played a chord that he thought was wrong and had a moment of panic, but Miles then just played a note right next to one Herbie played and made the mistake sound like something good. That's what I'm always hoping for with the people I play with. We rescue each other. If everybody's afraid they're going to make a mistake, or if they're keeping score, it's the worst feeling. But if everybody just feels like 'I'm just going to see what happens and go down that road' and if they maybe start to feel 'Oh, God, I'm going to fall off,' then everybody else can come in and pick you up. And if everybody's doing that all the time, and everybody is trusting each other and feeling safe, then you can take these chances. And that's the place I want to be."

"A friend asked me how I would describe the way you play music," I told Bill. "That was a tall order, and I didn't know how to verbalize it, but I recently read a book about cubism, and there are two statements in it that seemed to me to suggest an answer, and I wonder what you think of them. Picasso said: 'Cubism is not a reality you can take in your hand. It's more like a perfume, in front of you, behind you, to the sides, the scent is everywhere but you don't quite know where it comes from.'"

"That's great," Bill said, "and I think that's a pretty good description of what I'm trying to get close to and what I'm after."

"And Jacques Lipchitz stated: 'Cubism is like standing at a certain point on a mountain and looking around. If you go higher, things will look different. If you go lower, again they will look different. It's a point of view.'"

"And that's true for music too," Bill agreed. "Every which way you turn you're going to hear something different."

"Regarding your musical point of view—or views—about John Lennon's songs," I said, "I wanted to ask you about your 2011 album *All We Are Saying* . . . How did it come about?"

"Like so many things I do," Bill told me, "things just come my way, and I just follow them. What happened was that in the fall of 2005 we had a European tour set up and our first gig was going to be at the Cité de la Musique in Paris. This concert coincided with the opening of an exhibition they were presenting there to commemorate the twenty-fifth anniversary of John Lennon's death, so they asked us—it was just me, Jenny Scheinman, and Greg Leisz—if we could present an evening of Lennon songs. We prepared some of his songs before we left, got to Paris a day early and rehearsed them, and then played them at the concert, and loved doing them. And that's what started it. And our next gig was in Berlin, and we didn't say anything to anybody about what we were going to be playing, we just started doing the Lennon songs, and it wasn't until about a half hour into the concert that people began to realize that we were going to be playing nothing but Lennon music. And for the rest of the tour we only played Lennon.

"Then in 2011 we decided to make *All We Are Saying* . . . and we added Tony Scherr and Kenny Wollesen to the trio and recorded it at Fantasy Studios in Berkeley. Everybody had their own history with the songs, and I didn't make any arrangements, I didn't try to change anything. It was just each person's voice playing what they knew and remembered of those songs *together*. I didn't tell anybody what to do. It was either Duke Ellington or Jack DeJohnette who said that if you put a band together and have to tell them what to do, you've got the wrong people in the band. It's kind of a terrible feeling if someone is shadowing you all the time. You want it to be a dialogue, and I never tell anybody in my band what to do. I just have them there because I want to get close to what they have to say and learn from them.

"By the way, I should mention that because I did a John Lennon album doesn't mean that I don't love Paul too. I didn't mean for it to be that I'm on one side or the other [*laughing*]. Not at all. That was the furthest thing from my mind. It's just that I was asked to play John's music for that French concert, and the record was a result of our having played his music throughout our tour. And whenever I go back and listen to Paul's songs, there's more and more revealed. I was recently playing 'The Fool on the Hill,' which is deceptively simple and very subtle and very beautiful."

"Paul's also a great bass player," I said.

"It's crazy," Bill agreed, "what he does on the bass is so radical. My appreciation for Paul is enormous. Last year I saw the Rick Rubin conversations-with-Paul documentary miniseries [*McCartney 3,2,1*]. They're listening and talking about all of these McCartney songs, and their genius level is through the roof. He knows every little thing about his songs. I mean, I never listen to any of my records, I can't remember what I did, but Paul remembers the microscopic parts of each of them. And you can see how deep those songs work."

"You didn't include 'Strawberry Fields Forever' on your *All We Are Saying . . .* CD," I pointed out to Bill, "but over the years you've played it in many concerts with various musicians, and you also recorded an acoustic guitar version of the song during the *All We Are Saying . . .* sessions, and this Bonus Track can be found on several streaming services. To me, this acoustic version is one of the most profound, heart-piercing, and exquisite things you've ever done."

"Every time I play 'Strawberry Fields,'" Bill confessed, "it's like I'm discovering it for the first time, but at the same time the idea is that I'm hoping to just get past the edge of what I already know. I don't re-member specifically where it was that I first heard 'Strawberry Fields,' but it conjures up all kinds of smells and tastes and things that were going on at that time. It's been in my blood for so long, but even still, I didn't really know it, and there are all these steps I have to go through— I spent years learning how to read music, so I look at these little dots on the sheet music so that I know where to put my fingers, but you have to connect that with the place where the song becomes part of you. And I try to get to that point where I'm not thinking about the written notes, and every time I play the song I'm hoping to just get past the edge of what I already know. It keeps expanding, like a kaleidoscope or a rainbow, and each note of the melody and each chord opens up all kinds of new worlds."

"The French anthropologist Claude Lévi-Strauss stated that 'the in-vention of melody is the supreme mystery in the sciences of man.'"

"To me, the melody *is* the architecture," Bill affirmed, "and everything springs from that. The melody is the god, but it takes me a while to get it, it's deep down, but when you do, then these other things start springing from it. It's what sets me free when I play."

"Michelangelo," I mentioned, "famously said, 'I saw the angel in the marble and carved until I set him free.' And the folk singer Jean Ritchie said: 'The lovely past was not gone—it had just been shut up inside a song.' When you play, it sometimes seems to me that you're actually lib-erating or recovering the melody in a song."

"It's like you hear a pre-existing melody for the first time and go *wow*," Bill explained, "or maybe it doesn't get to you the first time. But with a lot of the best melodies you need to keep coming back to them—they're in your memory, but you have to go down deep enough to be in that same place where those things that you think are your own come from. But as I get older, I sometimes wonder, Am I just remembering something or am I inventing it?"

"Pete Seeger," I mentioned, "said that his father once compared truth to a rabbit in a bramble patch, and believed that you couldn't lay your hand on it. All you could do was to circle around it and point and say 'It's in there somewhere.' In your case, could you say that melody is in there but you can't get hold of it completely?"

"[*Laughing*] But I think you can. I hear what he's saying, and you may get scratched up a little bit, but it's definitely in there."

"In a 2014 interview you did with the *Atlantic,* you remarked: 'As I get older, I'm becoming more and more comfortable with the idea of playing something that was part of my life. Some naïve melody or childhood memory that I once would have thought wasn't complicated enough.' What did you mean by that?"

"There was a time early on when I was worried about what people would think or whether I wasn't being cool enough, but there came a point eventually when I realized that it was stupid not to be honest. For instance, I would secretly like a Burt Bacharach song on the radio, and I'd think, That's beautiful but that's too corny [*laughing*]. But as I've gotten older and recognize the genius in those songs, I'm no longer afraid to acknowledge it."

"One of my favorite songs," I told him, "is 'What the World Needs Now Is Love,' which Bacharach composed the music for."

"You know, I play that song almost every night, and I think, How could I have been so critical of this? I mean, just looking at it as a musical structure, there's some really crazy stuff going on there. You can think that something is too simple, but then you keep looking at it. It's like what John Cage said: 'If you think something is boring after two minutes, try it for four. If still boring, then eight. Then sixteen. Then thirty-two. Eventually one discovers that it's not boring at all.'"

JONATHAN F. P. ROSE

Bliss was it in that dawn to be alive,
But to be young was very heaven!
    —William Wordsworth

Jonathan F. P. Rose is a visionary polymath—an urban planner and developer of affordable and mixed-income housing; a leader in the green building and social justice communities; and the author of *The Well-Tempered City: What Modern Science, Ancient Civilizations, and Human Nature Teach Us about the Future of Urban Life,* an overarching examination of the city throughout history. In 2003 he cofounded the Garrison Institute in Garrison, New York, which focuses on the practical application of contemplative practices for addressing issues of civil society and the environment. In the 1980s he also had a career as a record producer for his label Gramavision Records, which specialized in jazz and new music recordings by musicians such as Anthony Davis, Bill Frisell, Jamaaladeen Tacuma, La Monte Young, and the Kronos Quartet; and throughout it all he has played bass and harmonica, most recently with his raga-jazz-blues band, Jog Blues.

I wanted to talk to Jonathan about the 1960s, when in many ways the Beatles' music acted as a unifying force throughout those fractured times, as well as about his own experiences of growing up in that era, and in early January 2022 we sat down to discuss this subject. I began by mentioning that I had recently finished reading a book called *Revolution in the Head: The Beatles' Records and the Sixties,* by the British music critic Ian MacDonald, in which he declares: "Anyone unlucky enough not to have been aged between 14 and 30 during 1966–7 will never know the excitement of those years in popular culture." And I pointed out to Jonathan that those were the years of "Penny Lane" and "Strawberry Fields Forever" and *Sgt. Pepper's Lonely Hearts Club Band,* and that since he was born in 1952, he had gotten in just under the wire.

"I did," Jonathan said, laughing. "My introduction to the Beatles occurred when I was eleven years old and heard 'I Want to Hold Your Hand' on the radio for the first time—that was in December 1963, a month after John Kennedy was killed, and I remember thinking, 'I wish President Kennedy had lived to hear this.' That's how monumentally new the Beatles music was. I'd been listening to popular music ever since I was a little kid, but this was something completely different and completely overwhelming. Their music had an expansiveness to it, a happiness to it, a joyfulness to it, an innocence to it, and it was so transformational.

"I was given a transistor radio when I was three or four," he told me, "and I loved it and used to keep it by my bed. My mother would always make me take an afternoon nap, and I would turn the radio on really low so that she couldn't hear it, put it under my pillow, and listen. And I would listen to it at night when I was supposed to be sleeping."

"You remember listening to music on the radio when you were that young?"

"And not only to music, but I also remember listening to daytime radio talk show commentators such as Galen Drake. He had interesting conversations, and he'd give advice and tell stories. And then as I got a little older, I would tune in to the 50,000-watt clear-channel stations, which were the most powerful AM stations, with no other ones on their frequencies, so that they could reach halfway across America. The radio was a gateway to different worlds. I remember stations from Wheeling, West Virginia, Chicago, and Detroit and some southern stations as well. I would hear different regional musics, ranging from Black music to country. And you could hear surfer culture too—I really loved the surf rock song 'Pipeline' by the Chantays, which came out when I was ten years old. 'Pipeline' could only have come out of California, and a song like 'Under the Boardwalk,' which I heard later on, could only have come out of New York. So there were these very distinctive sounds that opened into very distinctive worlds.

"I would also listen to Yankee games—visualizing the game through the voice of the announcer and the roar or murmur of the crowds—the baseball announcer would exclaim 'He winds up, and it's a *strike!*' And I don't know why, but when I was eight or nine I became fascinated by the Indianapolis 500 radio broadcasts—'Now stay tuned for the greatest spectacle in racing! It's lap 150, and Richard Petty is in the lead!' I could sit for hours listening to the sound of cars running around in circles! Also, my mother had the kitchen radio on WQXR, which played classical music. But mostly I was listening to Top 40 radio. So when the Beatles' first single came out, I had a pretty good perspective on how it compared to the popular music of the time.

"In the years before they recorded 'I Want to Hold Your Hand,' the Beatles had gone off to Germany where they played in Hamburg clubs that were pretty rough, so these were not innocent guys, but they came back and projected this sense of innocence and delight—they were apostles of good cheer, and that was exactly what society wanted and needed at that time. Musically, there was the rest of the world, and then there were the Beatles."

"The musician Steve Van Zandt," I mentioned to Jonathan, "once compared the impact of the Beatles to 'a spaceship landing in Central Park.'"

"Right. When 'I Want to Hold Your Hand' was recorded, John was twenty-three, Paul was twenty-one—they were so young and they were asked to be so much by the media and their fans. Their music evolved very quickly, they became this astonishing and phenomenal musical and cultural force. The progression from *Meet the Beatles* to *Sgt. Pepper's* was extraordinary, and took just three years.

"The midsixties was a time of enormous shifts—1966–1967 was a critical transitional time culturally, economically, and musically. When 'Strawberry Fields' and 'Penny Lane' were written, recorded, and released, the United States was becoming increasingly divided . . . and Europe too. For example, Detroit had a population of 1.6 million people in 1960. It was 73 percent white. By 1970, it was only 50 percent white and on its way to becoming 90 percent Black. America became increasingly suburban. Its urban, rural, and suburban cultures moved further apart. And this divide was reflected in the gap between generations and worldviews—those for and against the Vietnam War, those who were more and those who were less concerned that we were destroying the environment, for and against overcoming racism. You could really feel the split."

"And musically things were also in transition," I said.

"Yes, just look at Top 40 radio. According to one Top 40 Singles chart from December 10, 1966, when the Beatles were in the studio, the Beach Boys' 'Good Vibrations' was the number one single in America, in some ways laying out a challenge as to what could be done in songwriting and the studio. From the production point of view, 'Good Vibrations' was divided into segments, movements, almost like a symphony, there wasn't just a 4/4 beat all the way through it. And the theremin produced an eerie, out-of-the-world sound that people hadn't heard on pop radio before.

"Number two was Donovan's 'Mellow Yellow'—a kind of wry, simple drug-influenced song. Number three was the New Vaudeville Band's 'Winchester Cathedral'—a fairly trivial pop song. Number four was Mitch Ryder's 'Devil with a Blue Dress On'—pure rock and roll—and number five was the Supremes' 'You Keep Me Hanging On.' These reflected two sides of Detroit, the working-class white side and the aspirational Black side."

"And then there was FM radio," I added.

"In the 1960s," Jonathan reminded me, "the FM side of radio was the voice of the counterculture. In San Francisco you had the Grateful Dead and Big Brother and the Holding Company and Jefferson Airplane, a much more psychedelic music. And although it never made it on the charts, one of my favorite records from 1966 was the Paul Butterfield Blues Band's *East-West*, which included a thirteen-minute-long jam called 'East-West'—a transformation of Chicago blues and jazz into modal, half-Indian, half-Western improvisation that was completely antithetical to Top 40 radio. All of this was definitely music for a younger, hipper, countercultural 'us' who was not 'them'—those who would be listening to Roger Williams's 'Born Free' and Frank Sinatra's 'That's Life,' which were numbers eight and ten on the Top 40 Singles chart. And of course this 'us' versus 'them' divide persists and undermines American society today."

"But there were other divides as well, weren't there?"

"Yes, along with a deepening divide about the war in Vietnam, there was also a deepening divide about how to dress and how long to wear your hair. There was a generation gap and a spiritual gap, with the Beatles looking Eastward, and many Americans looking more toward the evangelical Billy Graham. And into this gap, the Beatles released 'Strawberry Fields Forever' and 'Penny Lane'—a double A-side single that transcended that gap. During a time that increasingly asked 'Which side are you on?,' they answered by dissolving the sides. Carl Schorske observed that what made Vienna great at the turn of the nineteenth century was that it had one foot in nostalgia and one foot in prophecy. The Beatles accomplished that."

"The writer Susan Sontag," I said, "once observed that 'the two poles of distinctively modern sentiment are nostalgia and utopia. Perhaps the most interesting characteristic of the time now labeled the sixties was that there was so little nostalgia. In that sense, it was indeed a utopian moment.'"

"I think that Sontag is right in general," Jonathan replied, "but to me a song like 'Penny Lane' runs counter to that idea because it's a very nostalgic song. Its characters—a barber, a fireman, a banker, and a nurse selling poppies—wouldn't be showing up on Carnaby Street at that time, nor in San Francisco during the Summer of Love or Greenwich Village. And remember that some of British fashion in the sixties was very 'Edwardian,' so there was this persistent reuse of nostalgia, although perhaps more so in Britain than America. The Penny Lane characters are from Paul McCartney's and John Lennon's youth, and the song depicted a postwar, very local English culture that was actually in decline."

"I interviewed John Lennon in 1968," I mentioned, "and he told me: 'We really got into the groove of imagining Penny Lane—the bank was there, and that was where the tram sheds were and people waiting and the inspector stood there, the fire engines were down there. It was just reliving childhood.'"

"Can you imagine the Grateful Dead or the Doors writing songs about where they grew up?" Jonathan asked me.

"Or," I added, "can you imagine Janis Joplin waxing nostalgic about her childhood in Port Arthur, Texas?"

"Right. The counterculture was, in general, making an abrupt break with its past. Its major capitals—in New York's Greenwich Village and San Francisco's Haight-Ashbury—were historically tight-knit immigrant communities that had inexpensive real estate and were full of charac-ter. Both escaped threatened demolition so that new freeways could run through them. These neighborhoods, and others like them around the country, became the soil in which the counterculture could gather and grow its aspiration to give birth to a new and better world. In 1968, a year after the nostalgic 'Penny Lane' was released, the Jefferson Airplane's Grace Slick sang her bandmate Paul Kantner's song 'Crown of Creation' on the TV show *The Smothers Brothers Comedy Hour.* The song described a sharp societal division, with the words 'In loyalty to their kind they cannot tolerate our minds. / In loyalty to our kind, we cannot tolerate their obstruction.' Slick ended the song by raising her fist, mimicking a Black Power salute.

"To be clear, the forward edge of American music often incorporated American folk music and the blues, and the urban counterculture had a vibrant, rural, even nostalgic back-to-the-land sibling. And although there were biographical songs, such as Bob Dylan's 'Girl from the North Country,' it wasn't typical for songwriters in their twenties—Ray Davies of the Kinks is one of the exceptions—to write about people like Eleanor Rigby and Father McKenzie or a banker with a motorcar. And what's significant is that 'Penny Lane' painted a picture of a wide range of very normal English people but did so with respect and humor. In the fractured world of the gap, there was a growing disrespect for people on the other side. 'Penny Lane' is the antithesis of 'othering.' It has compassion for its subjects. It heals the divides.

"'Strawberry Fields,' which was a darker song, invites the listener to join John Lennon on a journey and to share in his uncertainties. He's searching and trying to figure out something that he's unclear about. People of enormous popular significance are supposed to be icons of 'I've got it all figured out.' In 'Strawberry Fields,' Lennon exposed his personal vulnerability and is willing to publicly say, 'I don't really know, it could be this, it could be that, I'm not sure.' Musically it was complex, deep, and mirrored his uncertainty. It featured classical instruments, a very present electric guitar, and a Mellotron. The song pushed the capacities of the four-track recorder to its max and expanded the boundaries of what was considered to be popular music as well. The daring production techniques of 'Strawberry Fields' and 'Penny Lane' were prophetic and portended future albums like their own *Sgt. Pepper's Lonely Hearts Club Band* as well as albums by other rock groups. So it's that mixture of nostalgia and prophecy that I find very interesting. The stories of 'Penny Lane' and 'Strawberry Fields Forever' remind me of the title of William Blake's *Songs of Innocence and of Experience.*"

"Of course there's another side to the Beatles too," I pointed out. "In the film *A Hard Day's Night* a reporter asks Ringo if he's a Mod or a Rocker, and he answers, 'I'm a Mocker.'

"The Beatles were great mockers of the uptight society which they, like so many other young people at the time, felt they didn't fit into. And in your book *The Well-Tempered City* you quote an amazing statement by the literary critic Kenneth Burke, who declared: 'People may be unfitted by being fit in an unfit fitness.'"

"Let me explain that in the following way," Jonathan responded. "I grew up in a very stable family in a very comfortable little suburb, and I had everything I needed."

"Especially your transistor radio!" I interjected.

"Especially that. And yet I felt out of place and out of joint as many people in our generation did. Others, however, didn't feel that way, and that was actually another part of the divide we talked about before. But in the sixties many of us felt as if we were living in an unfit fitness; the predominant constructed social realm was out of alignment with the principles of nature and justice. We felt that the society ethos was misconstructed because it was doing violence to the environment and other peoples.

"People become unfitted if you ask them to fit into an unfit fitness, and here was a generation that was rebelling against that unfitness. But at the same time the generation was saying, 'We're actually fitted into something else, into this emerging counterculture that feels like home to us, a place where our spirits, minds, hearts, and music live. We're creating something else that feels much more fit for us.' It was a rejection and a movement away from the unfit fitness. There was an attempt to create and be part of a burgeoning, collaborative, idealistic, utopian world. The *Whole Earth Catalog* was its new encyclopedia. The Beatles may not have been able to be physically present in the ongoing creation of this world, but they provided its soundtrack."

"One of the other things about the Beatles that I find unique," I remarked, "is the way they seem to embody and convey both in their music—especially with their ecstatic and tender three-part vocal harmonizing—and also in their collective persona a sense of commonality and communality, manifested, for instance, in the song 'Girl' in which John, along with Paul and George, sighs 'Ah, *Girll*,' followed by a profound and slow inhalation of breath. They took breath together, and to use a beautiful phrase from your book *The Well-Tempered City*, they seem to have shared 'a common language of entwinement.' What exactly do you mean by entwinement?"

"I use the word *entwinement* to describe the deep fitness that pervades the universe, in which everything is connected and has exquisitely co-evolved. For example, there's the idea of quantum entanglement, which posits that there can be particles that are so interrelated that even if they are on different sides of the universe, if one rotates 180 degrees, the other rotates 180 degrees too. Ecologies are deeply entwined, with every element both creating the conditions of that ecosystem's evolution and being affected by those conditions. So the word connotes deep interconnectedness, and it conveys a sense of nurturing interconnectivity. And entwinement has this intimacy built into the word itself."

"In 'I Am the Walrus,'" I pointed out, "John Lennon sings: 'I am he as you are he as you are me / And we are all together.' And in her book *Sacred Therapy* the psychologist Estelle Frankel writes: 'When we join together as a collective, something greater constellates than the simple sum of individuals. Joined together, we atone for one another, for what one of us may lack another makes up for, and one person's weakness may evoke another strength. In community, then, we find our wholeness and healing.' To me, the four Beatles seemed to comprise a little collective, living aboard their yellow submarine, playing their joyous and healing music for all of us."

"And your quote from Estelle Frankel is a beautiful example of entwinement," Jonathan added.

"You yourself," I said, "are not only, among many other things, an urban developer and writer but also the founder of a musical group called Jog Blues, comprising a sitar, bass clarinet, electric guitar, cello, drums, tabla, vocalist—and you, like Paul McCartney, play the bass and harmonica. By the way, when did you start playing the bass?"

"I started playing bass when I started playing in bands because the other guys were better guitar players than me. Someone had to be the bass player, and it was the best role for me, and then I really got into playing bass, and I started playing harmonica after hearing James Cotton, viscerally feeling the South Side of Chicago in his sound. When I listen to music, I always listen to the bass part to hear what the bass player is doing. Paul often was playing what we think of as the lead part, or a counterharmony to the lead, on the bass. It was unusual in rock and roll, more akin to the way that Bach wrote music."

"In *The Well-Tempered City* you write: 'The essence of humans and nature has not changed. We feel a great sense of peace and joy when our minds are bounded by the synchrony of music, beauty, truth, dignity, love, and compassion.' What are the threads that weave the fabric of your own unbounded life?"

"The architect Christopher Alexander once said: 'Making wholeness heals the maker.' So if I had to take all the things I do together and say what is the mission of my life, I would say that it's to try to understand wholeness and make wholeness, and by doing that it becomes part of my own healing. There's a Jewish phrase, *Tikkun Olam,* that describes the human mission as to repair the fabric that has been torn asunder. It was the humans who had torn it asunder. Nature was doing just fine before us."

"That reminds me of the Latin phrase *natura sanat*—nature heals," I said.

"Yes, the nature of nature is to heal. There's a propensity toward healing and wholeness that is inherent in life and in nature, but we've constructed societies and communities that are running counter to this. And you see this in the way we treat each other and the earth. So in my work one of my goals is to figure out how to create more wholeness and try to heal the divides of inequality of opportunity, as well as to heal and repair the tears in nature and humans. Everything I do aspires to the idea of entwinement, and that's also what we try to do in music.

"The goal of Jog Blues is to bring together Indian raga, jazz, and blues, which are three of my musical loves, and weave them into one whole fabric by combining composition and improvisation. Composition represents the structure and organization of the world—and we've been talking about how Beatles songs like 'Strawberry Fields' and 'Penny

Lane,' for example, are so exquisitely composed—it's something amazing that the human mind can do—and improvisation is creating the conditions for freedom, in which something inspirational emerges. Improvisation requires a tremendous amount of listening and attention. We live in a world that's endlessly seeking to capture our attention for commercial or political use. When making music, we can apply our collective attention, the attention of the musicians and the audience, to listening to each other, supporting each other, harmonizing with each other, unleashing each other, and generating joy."

"The great jazz musician and composer Ornette Coleman," I told Jonathan, "when speaking about the members of his band, famously remarked: 'I don't want them to follow me, I want them to follow themselves, but to *be* with me.'"

"And that," said Jonathan, "is the right way to play music and the right way to live."

MARGARET KLENCK

The seat of the soul is there where
the inner and outer worlds meet.
   —Novalis

In September 1968 I interviewed John Lennon in London for *Rolling Stone* magazine, and during the interview I mentioned to him that a lot of my friends liked to sit around and analyze his songs.

"Well, they *can* take them apart," he told me.

"And you don't mind that?" I asked, surprised.

"Surely not," he said. "I mean, I hit it on all levels, you know. I write lyrics, and you don't realize what they mean till after. Especially some of the better songs or some of the more flowing ones, like 'Walrus.' The whole first verse was written without any knowledge. And 'Tomorrow Never Knows'—I didn't know what I was saying, and you just find out later. It's really like abstract art. When you have to think about it to write it, it just means that you've labored at it. But when you just *say* it, man, it's a continuous flow. The same as when you're recording or just playing— you come out of a thing and you know *I've been there*—it's just pure, and that's what we're really looking for all the time. So when there are some lyrics of mine that I dig, I know that somewhere people will be looking at them. And so the people who analyze the songs—good on 'em, because they work on all levels. So I don't mind what they do with them."

John Lennon once described "Strawberry Fields Forever" as "psycho-analysis set to music," and because I was planning to write a book about "Strawberry Fields Forever" and "Penny Lane," I decided to get in touch with Margaret Klenck, a Jungian Analyst in private practice in New York City and past president of the Jungian Psychoanalytic Association of New York. In 2016, when I was working on a book about Maurice Sendak's children's picture book *Outside Over There,* I had conversed with Margaret about Sendak's story of a nine-year-old girl named Ida who descends into an underground grotto in order to rescue her baby sister from goblins who had abducted and imprisoned her. I had found Margaret's insights regarding that book to be revelatory, so I once again contacted her and mentioned that I was going to be writing about "Strawberry Fields Forever" and "Penny Lane" and wondered if she might have time to discuss those songs with me. She agreed to do so, and when I phoned her to set up an appointment, she said: "You know, those two songs were always important to me because aside from being wonderful rock and roll songs, they also messed with one's soul and pulled one into all kinds of existential questions that I was asking when I was a young person about identity and about how to relate to the world of grownups. There's a lot to say about both of those songs."

I met up with Margaret in January 2022 at her Upper West Side office and asked if we could first discuss "Strawberry Fields Forever," which, among other things, seemed to be a quintessential example of free association set to music, and I quoted to her the psychoanalyst Sándor Ferenczi's statement that "the patient is not cured by free-associating, he is cured when he *can* free-associate."

"In Jungian analysis," Margaret told me, "we don't use the technique of free association very much, but I think that what Ferenczi is saying is that once your imagination and your relationship to yourself is freed up, then you can heal. Free association is a willingness to see the pattern of your life, and once you're in touch with yourself you can get to know yourself."

"That's what I think John Lennon is trying to do in 'Strawberry Fields Forever,'" I said, "but I want to find out what you think about this, so perhaps we could start off our discussion by taking a look at the first stanza of the song."

And I read aloud:

> Let me take you down
> 'Cos I'm going to Strawberry Fields
> Nothing is real
> And nothing to get hung about
> Strawberry Fields forever

"Right from the outset, John's inviting us to join him on a journey."

"He's going to go inward," Margaret agreed, "he's going to go backward, he's going into memory, he's going to go into whatever Strawberry Fields is to him, and he wants you to come along with him.

"When I first heard this song as a young person," she added, "I felt that I was being invited to companion John, but that was a romantic idealization. I thought he was in fear and despair and he needed a companion to be with him in places that were too crazy for him. I've always heard this as an invitation, but the analyst in me also hears it as the outline of depression—this is the way depression speaks itself. Of course it isn't the only way to see this, but perhaps I can elaborate on that later. I want to make clear, however, that it would be wrongheaded of me to attempt to analyze John Lennon, but I'll accept his invitation to look at his song freely with what I know and who I am."

"To me, Strawberry Fields is the underworld," I said, "and John wants to go down there, just like Lewis Carroll's Alice who, 'burning with curiosity,' wants to follow the White Rabbit down the rabbit hole. 'Down went Alice after it,' Lewis Carroll writes, 'never once considering how in the world she was going to get out again.' The Alice books were two of John's most favorite childhood books, and it's interesting that Lewis Carroll's original title for *Alice's Adventures in Wonderland* was *Alice's Adventures Under Ground*."

"That's perfect," Margaret said, "but the difference is that Alice doesn't know where she's going, whereas John kind of knows where he's going because he's been there before. Strawberry Fields is certainly a reference to the Strawberry Field of his childhood, which was the Salvation Army orphanage he loved to visit and explore as a child. If we put this in dream terms, then we can say that if somebody has an image in a dream that's closely related to an image in their waking life it's usually connected; there's going to be some kind of bridge to the dream. And as I see it, Strawberry Fields isn't an imaginary place like Alice's Wonderland, it's not the Elysian Fields, it's specific to a literal place in John's childhood. I think that for him it was a place of joyful transgression and it was an enticement. He would jump the wall and sneak into the garden, and often with his pals. There was some fearfulness because it was an orphanage, and it was forbidden, and his aunt Mimi would admonish him that if he didn't stop doing that they would hang him. But it was a magical place, a place where he seemed to feel free, there really was nothing to get hung about, and in the garden party that took place there every summer the Salvation Army band would play, and music was his salvation. So when John invites us to come down to Strawberry Fields—with the added 's'—I think he's saying: I've been there and you're going to like it. It's a place that pulls on all of those images and has become a place in his interior that he can go to, a place of meeting himself. There seems to be something special about Strawberry Field and his experience of and longing for it—the Salvation Army and perhaps his fear and fascination with the orphans—because he came to know himself there. It touched something in him that he never forgot."

"But it's a place in his imagination," I noted.

"Well, it's *all* in his imagination," Margaret said, "but it's not an imaginary place like Alice's Wonderland, it's an amplification of a literal place—Strawberry Field—that seems to have been a good place for him, that combined all those things that were so important to him. But Strawberry Fields is the underworld without question, although what it means to him is one thing and what it means to everyone else who listens to the song is another thing. It's going to have to do with their own relationships to their own undergrounds.

"Everybody's got a Strawberry Fields in them, a special place where something becomes clear to them about themselves, where they get to enact themselves in a new way and have a freedom that they've never felt before. And what makes this song so universal is that everybody knows that feeling of going to a place that has meaning for them. It could be a religious thing, it could be a prayer thing. A memory place. It's down and in, and everyone's got one."

"So it's like home."

"I don't think it's home," Margaret disagreed. "I think that one of the things that makes Strawberry Fields special is that it isn't home, it's actually the place where you're defying family. The aunt's not here, the mother's not there—there aren't any parents there. It's an orphanage, so to speak. We all have places where we get to know ourselves outside our family complex, those places where we first discover that we are more than just our family, where we feel untethered and can grow up and do something completely different from our family and still survive and find that people still like us."

"What you're saying," I said, "reminds me of the passage in the Book of Genesis where God says to Abraham 'Go to yourself'—lech lecha in Hebrew—'and leave your homeland, your birthplace, your parents' house, and go to the land that I will show you.'"

"And that's why John goes down to Strawberry Fields," Margaret commented, "because I feel that it's a defining place for him where he can get in touch with himself, and you can get to that place anywhere. You don't have to be in Liverpool, you can do it in Spain where he wrote the song. He's talking about an inner place where he's himself."

"The fifteenth-century Indian poet Kabir wrote: 'Wherever you are is the entry point.'"

"That's exactly what I'm suggesting," she said. "There are these events in a life that accumulate into a personality, into a sense of self, and to me it's pretty clear that Strawberry Field and John's experiences there as a child were important in a profound archetypal way. It was the place where it seems he came to know himself, and he defined himself by that."

"It's interesting," I told Margaret, "that when I interviewed John Lennon in London in 1968 he said to me 'Strawberry Fields is anywhere you want to go.'"

"And I think the operative word here is *want*—what is your desire? Where are you going to find yourself? And John says 'anywhere you want to go' is where you're going to find yourself, somewhere that's syntonic, somewhere that's resonant with you. Therefore Strawberry Fields is filled with desire, it's a desirous place, and once you've engaged your passion and know that you want to go, you can go there."

"And he's inviting us to go with him."

"That's right—come along and let me take you, because once you want to go somewhere you can do it too."

"And do so without fear."

"Right. It's not real, it's memory, it's nothing to get upset about, it's filled with archetypal experience. And archetypes are forever."

"But inviting us to go with him," I pointed out, "seems to me to be a bit of a paradox, since this is something that we need to do on our own. It's like the song 'Lonesome Valley': 'You gotta walk that lonesome valley / Nobody here can walk it for you / Ya gotta walk it by yourself.'"

"What I think John's saying," Margaret explained, "is: Let me show you it can be done, you're not going to get hanged, there's nothing to get hung about, and that whenever you want to go inward and go to a place that's meaningful to you internally, you can do it too. But I also think that our undergrounds *can* be shared—in art, in theater, in our empathy and sympathy with the world. Think of those medical people who work twenty-hour shifts in hospitals filled with Covid patients. Those people share their undergrounds, they're really digging into their suffering in order to be able to do the work. We don't always have to be alone, but we still have to 'go to ourselves.'"

"The second-century Christian author Tertullian," I mentioned, "wrote about Christ's harrowing of hell, and Tertullian stated: 'It was for this purpose that Christ descended into hell so that we ourselves might not have to descend thither.' According to this idea, Jesus does it for us so we don't have to make that inner journey. He's not inviting us to go down with him."

"That's the idea of salvation," Margaret said. "He's saying, I'm doing it for you so you don't have to go to hell, I'm making the sacrifice once and for all so you don't have to be sacrificed. I am the sacrificial lamb so you don't have to be burned on the altar. But his teachings are still hard, and he doesn't let you off."

"Tertullian was a polemicist against heresy," I noted, "including Christian gnosticism, but the gnostics took a different view of this. In the Gospel of Thomas Jesus says: 'If you bring forth what is within you, what you bring forth will save you. If you do not bring forth what is within you, what you do not bring forth will destroy you.'"

"That going in and discovering your truth," she told me, "is part of the task of bringing forth. It's a deep dive, but you've got to bring it forth, you've got to love, you've got to save the earth. Jung said that individuation isn't complete until you bring it back into the world. That's the only way to heal."

"The Greek god Dionysus," I said, "descended into Hades twice—the first time was to redeem his mother Semele, but in his play *Frogs* Aristophanes tells us that the god's second trip to the underworld was in search of poetry to save the city. So maybe that's another reason why John Lennon went down to Strawberry Fields. He wanted to heal all of us!"

"That's a wonderful idea," Margaret said, smiling. "But if you're going into the unknown to try to discover your truth, you have to be willing to be undone a little bit by what you come upon. Because the unconscious is, as Jung stated, simply the unknown."

"In this regard," I said, "I'm reminded of the poet John Keats's notion of 'negative capability,' which he described as 'the ability to remain within mysteries, uncertainties, and doubt without the irritable reaching out after fact and reason.'"

"And you have to be able to tolerate that if you want to get to know yourself," Margaret affirmed. "Anna Freud talks about the restoration and defense of the ego, but that's a task that can also sometimes be a defense, because then you don't get to know the unknown."

"Alice was certainly an adept of negative capability," I remarked. "At one point she found herself falling down a very deep well, and Lewis Carroll tells us that as she went down, she had plenty of time to look about her and to wonder what was going to happen next. 'First she tried to look down and make out what she was coming to, but it was too dark to see anything.' The unknown is a very dark place, and I wanted to quote something to you from a fascinating book by Barbara Hurd called *Entering the Stone: On Caves and Feeling through the Dark*. In it she writes: 'Far below the light of the cave entrance, I think about Plato, wonder what it would mean if his myth were reversed. How might Western thinking have evolved differently if the man who broke his chains in the cave looked up toward the light but changed his mind, pivoted, went down instead, farther into the cave, deeper than the fire, down to where there's no light at all, beyond shadows where even the body seems to fade? What kind of knowledge might he bring back? What would it mean to be *endarkened*?'"

"That's beautiful," Margaret said, "and it's what we're talking about. It takes a strong sense of self to be able to be endarkened and not disappear, just as it takes a tremendous sense of self to be truly enlightened and not to be eaten up by the light as so many mystics were. But in this respect, the Jung in me wants to also say that Barbara Hurd's notion about going farther and farther in until there's no light can also be a retreat not only into the darkness but also into nonrelationality. There's nothing there except darkness. Just the way the moth goes to the flame and then there's nothing but flame. And as I said before, we always have to be able to come back.

"Have you ever been in one of those isolation tanks of water where it's completely dark and soundproof, and you're floating, and there's just enough salt so that you float without any effort? Some people experience that as a miraculous floating in the universe, and other people can't bear it because they've got nothing to relate to, their own minds can't hold themselves in mind and they can't tolerate it. But in 'Strawberry Fields Forever' John Lennon never loses a sense of self. It may be confused or filled with doubt, but he doesn't dissolve, he's not lost in the darkness, he's stumbling around but there's still light."

"Let's go on to the next stanza," I suggested.

> Living is easy with eyes closed
> Misunderstanding all you see
> It's getting hard to be someone
> But it all works out
> It doesn't matter much to me

"When we began our conversation," Margaret reminded me, "I mentioned that I also hear this song as an outline of depression."

"So you think that John Lennon is not only going down but is also feeling down?" I asked her.

"Let me explain what I mean by this, and thinking and talking about this stanza and the following one might be a good way to do that.

"The first line—'Living is easy with eyes closed'—is such a beautiful image of not being present, and if you close your eyes and aren't present you just live in your own little fantasy and stay on your own little hamster wheel."

"Herman Melville," I said, "took a different view of this, and wrote: 'No man can ever feel his own identity aright except his eyes be closed; as if darkness were indeed the proper element of our essences, though light be more congenial to our clayey part.' You know how when you're listening to music, for example, you sometimes close your eyes so that you can hear more intensely."

"And you're not distracted by everything else out there," Margaret added. "But I feel that John Lennon may be saying the opposite here. He's not noticing anything, he's not really there, his head's in the sand. Like an ostrich. In fact, he isn't feeling his identity aright at all. He says it's getting hard to be someone."

"There's a great passage in *Alice's Adventures in Wonderland*," I said, "that sounds to me like the way John Lennon might be feeling here. Alice is confused about who she is and is trying to get her bearings, and she imagines that she might be her friend Mabel. 'If I'm Mabel,' she says to herself, 'I'll stay down here! It'll be no use their putting their heads down and saying "Come up again, dear!" I shall only look up and say, "Who am I then? Tell me that first, and then if I like being that person, I'll come up: if not, I'll stay down here till I'm somebody else."'"

"It's interesting where you're going with this," Margaret commented. "I'd been going in the direction of, you know, he's been somebody, he's been John bloody Lennon, and has been the leader of the Beatles, and it's hard to be that someone now."

"In Spain," I told her, "he was being forced for the first time to think of what it would be like for him not to be a Beatle."

"And what it would be like to be a person, and to be a citizen of the world," she added. "The fact that you go to Alice is very instructive because your putting the two of them together suggests that he won't necessarily be John *Lennon*, he could be Mabel, he could be anybody. And if he's not John Lennon, who is he?"

"And that's exactly what the Caterpillar asked Alice," I pointed out: "'Who are *you*?' John once declared that 'the few true songs' he ever wrote were 'Help!' and 'Strawberry Fields Forever.' And in 'Help!' he confesses that when he was younger he never needed anybody's help, but he's no longer feeling so self-assured, and he's now feeling 'down' and insecure—

'My independence seems to vanish in the haze'—and he ends the song by pleading 'Won't you please, please help me, help me?' He later remarked that this song was a personal cry of anguish."

"And in 'Strawberry Fields,'" Margaret reminded me, "John says that nothing is real and that it's getting hard to be someone but that it all works out. But when he says 'It doesn't matter much to me,' I wonder, because I hear that more as 'It matters a *whole* lot to me, but I'm not going to acknowledge how much it means to me.'

"In my experience there are three kinds of depression. There's circumstantial depression, like when you've lost a job, and there's creative depression, which Jung and Freud both had—they fell apart and had to find out what was missing and bring it back up—and then there's chronic depression where there doesn't seem to be a way out. But I think that Strawberry Fields feels like a creative place for John, and when depression is creative, you make art, you go into yourself—you go down and under—and you find what you hadn't brought forth before, something that's been left behind that needs to get born. And, as with Alice, this is an adventuresome journey. But I still think that the tone here is one of depression, and to me, the third stanza also reflects that tone."

"Here's that stanza," I said, and read it aloud:

> No one I think is in my tree
> I mean it must be high or low
> That is you can't, you know, tune in
> But it's all right
> That is I think it's not too bad

"When John began to write this song," I told Margaret, "it had no chorus and only one verse, which began 'There's no one on my wavelength, / I mean it's either too high or too low,' and only later did he change 'wavelength' to 'tree.' And the title he originally gave to the song was 'It's Not Too Bad.'"

"That's it," Margaret said. "That's where I sense that depressive mood. 'But it's all right / That is I think it's not too bad' is so equivocal, so wondering and wandering and longing for it to be okay. You know how depression can come in like a wave, it doesn't have to be a big wave but it washes away whatever you've just drawn or built in the sand. You've got an idea and it starts to come together and then the wave just washes it away."

"But on the other hand," I noted, "it's like what happens when you're meditating and you have, say, a depressive thought, and you just see it and let it go. And perhaps that's what John's doing here. He has faith or at least a hope that it's going to work out."

"It could be," Margaret said, "and of course I know that this is just one way to read this, but when you're depressed and you come to the conclusion that it's all going to work out, the hope is in the *hope*, it doesn't mean that the depression is gone. And as I mentioned before, I personally hear his 'It doesn't matter much to me' and now his 'That is I think it's not too bad'—he doesn't say 'I *know*'—as classic depression. Because it matters a whole lot. When people begin to get really depressed, it's like 'it doesn't matter much and it's all right and I think it's not too bad.'"

"And of course," I said, "the stanza begins with the line 'No one I think is in my tree.'"

"I had a Danish patient many years ago," Margaret told me, "who would say, 'Nobody's in my tree,' and she said that it was a Danish expression."

"Meaning I'm alone up here."

"Yes, and John seems to be saying, 'I'm alone, I'm on my own wavelength, you can't tune in, nobody gets me.'"

"He's also saying that the tree is either high or low," I added, "but in either case you can't tune in no matter what level it's on. And I'm once again reminded of 'Help!' in which John pleads: 'Help me get my feet back on the ground / Won't you please, please help me.'"

"There's a loneliness thread that runs through these two stanzas," Margaret said, "but I also should point out that the 'you know' in the line 'That is you can't, you know, tune in' is so brilliant because it suggests that if you *do* know, maybe you might be able to tune in. I think it turns a little corner, there is some hope in there, and there's more of it in the next stanza."

"And that stanza," I said, "is astonishing":

> Always, no sometimes, think it's me
> But you know I know when it's a dream
> I think, I know, I mean a 'Yes'
> But it's all wrong
> That is I think I disagree

"In this stanza," I pointed out, "John Lennon uses the word *I* six times and the word *know* three times, with its play on the homonyms *know* and *no.*"

"The first thing I noticed," Margaret said, "was how the 'I' shifts from the way it was used in the previous stanza—there the 'I' was the one who was saying 'It's all right' or 'I think it's not too bad'—but now John's observing himself, and I think that he's completely lost in self-reference, which follows from his sense that nobody else gets him, nobody can tune in, and he can't tune in to himself."

"He's really fragmented."

"He's fragmented, but I would rather say that he's dissociated. From the Jungian perspective you could say that the ego complex isn't holding. He's in some other kind of state."

"Perhaps he's lucid dreaming. He's in a dream but he's aware that he's dreaming."

"It could be that," she said, "and it could also be the kind of thing that people talk about when they're tripping, which is that they know that they're tripping but they also know that they don't know that they are. I don't know what part of him is knowing what he knows, but maybe it is a lucid dream. I think that when he loses track of his sense of self, he tries to assure himself 'I know when it's a dream, I think, I know.' And then he says, 'But it's all wrong, that is I think I disagree.' The 'it' is the big question for me. Is it the state that he's in or is it that his understanding of himself is wrong? What's that 'it'?"

"How would you take it?"

"The darkest way to take 'it,'" Margaret suggested, "is to conclude that this whole trip to Strawberry Fields is wrong, that trying to get in touch with and trying to discover something about himself is kerflooey. But it's so confusing that you could take it any way you want to."

"Barbara Hurd," I noted, "wrote: 'Peel away the layers of an onion and what you get down to is something oblong and pearly, not a core, a seed, or a bone that says the beginning, but the last layer of succulence, a cluster of veined petals, a nest of opalescence.' And John himself wrote a song called 'Glass Onion' which begins: 'I told you about strawberry fields / You know the place where nothing is real.'"

"The onion is a good way to describe this sense of disintegration," Margaret agreed. "There's no center, the center isn't holding, even his thinking isn't holding. I feel that he's disintegrating in the way that one does in despair, in depression, on an LSD trip, when all of the external markers—the Beatles, the celebrity life—are falling away, the mirrors are all gone, the onion of him has been peeled."

"But in spite of his disintegration," I observed, "he's nevertheless looking for a 'Yes,' which is what he would soon find when he met Yoko Ono."

"Yes, he's looking for it, he's searching, like Orpheus going into the underworld to find Eurydice, to find love."

"James Hillman asserted that each dream is a step into the underworld."

"Hillman's right," Margaret said, "and you don't go there voluntarily or on a lark—you go to find your lost love, your truth, you go down there for soul. I think John Lennon was looking for the place that brought him comfort as a child, the place that helped define him as a rebellious kid who had fun and friends. And now he's confronted with who he is now— he wasn't searching when he was eleven, he was *living*."

"The psychoanalyst D. W. Winnicott," I mentioned, "wrote about the idea of unintegration, and he proposed that it is unhealthy to deny or fear 'the innate capacity of every human being to become unintegrated and to feel that the world is unreal.' And he believed that a person who had the capacity 'to be,' as opposed to one who can just 'do,' has the capacity to feel real."

"I agree, and Jung himself was one of the first people to say that the psyche is dissociable, each with dissociated parts and complexes, and that's health. If we can't dissociate we couldn't learn or grow. We're talking here about the disintegration of the ego, which is the house of consciousness, and if we couldn't dissociate and disintegrate, we couldn't survive much because we have to be able to find a way to take in what's happening at a frequency that we can tolerate. The classic examples are a rape or a car accident where the person sees themselves up on the ceiling, watching what's happening. If you didn't get to do that, you'd go mad. It's how people can get through wars."

"And in a way that's what John Lennon is doing here, isn't he?"

"I think that he's allowing himself to splinter," she explained. "I'd suggest that he's choosing to go to a place that is safe and filled with nourishment for him so that he can disintegrate a little bit and get in touch with his doubt and confusion and sorrow and fear and loneliness. And then he gets to the place of 'I know what I know but I don't know,' and it's a sacred place to be. It's like St. Thomas who's the saint of doubt. If we can't doubt, we can't go forward. John is totally in doubt and unsure. And then in that lovely final line 'That is I think I disagree' he's trying to coagulate."

"So you're saying that the 'I' at that moment is more unified than the fragmented 'I' from before."

"He was in pieces in the beginning of that stanza, but by the end of it he says he's able to disagree, and when you're able to disagree, it means you've been able to think about it."

"It's like the title of Mark Epstein's book *Going to Pieces without Falling Apart*."

"Yes, John is going to pieces and then he pulls it back together. It's a real struggle, he's really wrestling, and he's doing the thing that Jung teaches us to do which is to go *in*—you have an experience, you bring it up and you think about it. And John goes down and gets to that moment of 'It's getting hard to be someone' and comes back up with a little piece of coal, then looks at and thinks about it. And that is the model of analysis."

"So do you come back with new knowledge?"

"You come back with experience, it doesn't become knowledge right away. Knowledge is a continuation of experiences, thoughts, and feelings . . . and you also come back with images."

"Like Strawberry Fields," I said.

"Like Strawberry Fields. And knowledge is a hard-won thing."

"In his 'Auguries of Innocence,'" I mentioned to Margaret, "William Blake wrote: 'Under every grief & pine / Runs a joy with silken twine.' You've made me become aware, as I never had before, of the grief and pine expressed in 'Strawberry Fields Forever,' but I wonder if you find this a depressive song."

"Not at all," Margaret replied. "I think it's a very exciting song; it's got lots of solution in it. John Lennon had the courage to really allow his experience of disintegration and depression to be solved by going back and down to Strawberry Fields. He can get to the place where he's falling apart, and he uses his inner resources to get himself out of it. In the midst of his not knowing and his saying 'no' and 'it doesn't matter,' there's a yes in him—'I think, I know, I mean a yes.' It's an affirmation, and when he sees that yes he knows it's something true to him, and it's a strong, powerful model of how you can use all of your confusions and inner places to bring together all of the different parts of yourself. In 'Strawberry Fields Forever,' John Lennon goes to visit himself. He knows he's been there, he knows it's wherever he wants to be, and we can come too."

"I've gone down with you to Strawberry Fields," I said to Margaret, "and now I'd like to go up with you to Penny Lane. We've been in Hades and perhaps we could now spend a little bit of time in the realm of Hades's brother, Zeus, whom the Greeks called the Sky Father, the god of the luminous day sky, to whom Paul McCartney pays homage: 'Penny Lane is in my ears and in my eyes / There beneath the blue suburban skies.'"

"That's where Paul seems to identify," she told me, "up there in the above world, whereas in Strawberry Fields John identifies with the underworld."

"James Hillman," I said, "asserted that soul resides in Hades."

"But I would argue that soul resides in the above world as well," she said. "If somebody is deeply drawn to the depths, their shadow is going to be aboveground and they're not going to see themselves as joyful and related to the light. And someone who only sees themselves as joyful and related to the light is going to be afraid to go to the depths, so they're missing half their souls because soul has to be in both places. If you only have one, there's no differentiation. If there's all Zeus, then there's no darkness and no death.

"It all has to do with consciousness. Some people just want to live in the daylight with only happiness and smiley faces, they don't want to see any shadows anywhere, and that can make them pretty crazy. And for people who don't want to let any light in, that can make them miserable. So you see, it's about relationship. There has to be two to have a relationship. Without words like *inner* and *outer* or *above* and *below*, and without gods like Hades and Zeus, there can be no relationship. In all creation myths the first thing that happens is that there is a differentiation, an above and a below, and without differentiation there can be no self-knowledge, no encounter, and no more creation."

"In this context," I said, "one could also speak about yin and yang, but these opposite and sometimes contrary forces can actually be complementary, interconnected, and interdependent."

"But they're still two," Margaret pointed out, "and you can't be interdependent if you're only one. Consciousness splits things into two, but without twos there can't be consciousness, and there has to be an *other* in order for you to love. If it's pure merge, it's not love."

"The anthropologist Gregory Bateson once remarked: 'You have to know two to be one.'"

"That's right, and we all have these different parts of ourselves, all of the complexes, and they're in relationship to each other."

"The fact that Zeus and Hades are brothers," I observed, "seems to indicate that the upper and lower worlds are the same, but one brother views it from above and the other one views it from below."

"One of them is in charge of the outside," she said, "the other is in charge of the inside. They're defined by their different perspectives, and they need each other because if there was no light, there wouldn't be such a thing as dark. They rely on each other to exist."

"And couldn't one say the same about 'Penny Lane' and 'Strawberry Fields Forever'?" I asked. "They're in fact two sides of the same record."

"They are, and I think that they reflect the two sides of the way Paul and John experienced growing up in Liverpool. Paul talked about the different kinds of childhoods they had, their different kinds of motherings and fatherings—of course in John's case there was no fathering—and their different constitutions."

"The poet Rainer Maria Rilke wrote: 'Never believe that fate is more than the condensation of childhood.'"

"And you could perhaps say that's what both of these songs are about. Paul seems to have had a pretty happy and peaceful aboveground childhood, the world wasn't antagonistic toward him in the way that John's world was. He was the good kid, John was the rapscallion, and they helped define each other. It obviously wasn't conscious, but in any couple—if you might want to call them a couple in that way—there are these compensations: for instance, one person can be neater, the other sloppier, one person is more adventurous, the other more stay-at-home. And that's complementary in the yin-yang way that you referred to.

"Because for all of their differences, Paul and John both 'got' each other and were able to get on each other's wavelengths, otherwise they wouldn't have been able to work and create together. They balanced the tension of opposites, each one compensating for the lacuna in the other—Paul doesn't go down, and in 'Strawberry Fields Forever' John doesn't enjoy the suburban sunshine—and you can often hear the different strains of their personalities."

"A good example of that," I mentioned, "occurs in the Beatles' song 'Getting Better,' which was written mainly by Paul, but when he sang 'I've got to admit it's getting better / A little better all the time,' John leans in vocally and sardonically intones 'It can't get no worse.'"

"There you are, and that reveals the difference between the two of them. 'Penny Lane' is different from 'Strawberry Fields Forever,' so let me tell you what my overall feelings and impressions are about that song.

"In 'Strawberry Fields' nothing is solid, but 'Penny Lane' is all about solid. This is the upper world, the sunlight world, the world of Zeus, and this is the Queen's world, which is suggested by the dazzle of the piccolo trumpet solo at the end of the song, as opposed to the heavy cellos and brass that you hear in 'Strawberry Fields.'"

"John Lennon said that Strawberry Fields is anywhere you want to go," I said, "but 'Penny Lane' is not only solid but it's a very specific place. Paul once remarked that 'the characters in "Penny Lane" are still very real to me. I drive past it to this day, showing people the barbershop, the bank, the fire station, the church I used to sing in, and where the girl stood with the tray of poppies as I waited for the bus. I remember her vividly. . . . So it resonates in several ways: it's still 'in my ears and in my eyes.'"

"It's normal life," Margaret said, "and he remembers it viscerally. It's got what you need: you get your haircut, you go to the bank, you buy poppies from a tray. It's deeply ordinary *being*. This is a *being* song. These are the people who are keeping the world running, and they come and go and they stop and say hello. It's perpetual. There's a foreverness in this, and it's real life."

"John Lennon," I pointed out, "expressed his feeling that 'nothing is real,' but Paul's world seems to exemplify what the Cuban writer Alejo Carpentier called 'the marvelous real.'"

"And it's filled with light, and light is always connected with con-sciousness. Penny Lane kind of all makes sense except for some things that seem weird and strange from a child's point of view . . ."

". . . like the banker who never wears a mac in the pouring rain," I said, "or like the fireman who rushes into the barbershop. It's very strange, as Paul says, or, as Alice would say, 'Curiouser and curiouser.'"

"And Alice can say that," Margaret said, "because she has a place from which to observe things. One of the differences I felt about the two songs was that when John goes down to the underworld, there's no point of reference. But in the Zeus world everything has a point of reference, so when something's a little off, you can say that it's strange because you can always say something's strange if you have a point of reference."

"And it's strange," I remarked, "that in Penny Lane there are blue skies but it's also pouring rain, and the song takes place in spring but the pretty nurse is selling poppies on Remembrance Day, which takes place in late autumn. In a way it suggests T. S. Eliot's idea about time present and time past being present in time future, and time future contained in time past. Penny Lane is now in his ears and in his eyes, but he's also remembering it, and it's all mixed up."

"It's confused," Margaret agreed, "but it doesn't seem to unsettle him because this is just the way it is, and the oddness doesn't do more than perk his interest. It's a memory song, but you do get a sense of time in it, whereas in 'Strawberry Fields Forever' everything is happening in the moment, and time is completely gone."

"Speaking about time, the strangest line in 'Penny Lane' for me is 'In Penny Lane there is a fireman with an hourglass,' and I was astonished to find out that it was John who had suggested this image."

"The hourglass is a consciousness-raising implement," she observed, "because you have to turn it over and by doing so you're consciously par-ticipating in the movement of time. The hourglass keeps time in small increments, it's small chunks of time."

"'Penny Lane' lasts just a little over three minutes," I told her, "and

'Strawberry Fields Forever' lasts just a little over four minutes, and they're two sides of the same record."

"And similarly each of us has an inside and an outside," Margaret said, "and because there is an inside there can be an outside. If there's no inside and outside, what are we? They define each other, and this creates a wholeness. I think that 'Penny Lane' and 'Strawberry Fields Forever' create a wholeness, and I think that Penny Lane and Strawberry Fields serve as similar kinds of places for Paul and John, and what makes these songs so powerful is that they're psychologically so accurate. But we all have places like these within us—places that have a special meaning for us—and all we have to do is find them."

RICHARD GERE

Like a shooting star, a mirage, a flame, a magic trick, a dewdrop,
a water bubble, a dream—consider all things thus.
    —The Buddha

Richard Gere is a person of myriad accomplishments. He is an actor who has appeared in more than fifty films; a photographer whose book *Pilgrim*, published in 1997, consists of sixty-five black-and-white photographs of Tibet, its people, and its community in exile, which he took in Tibet, India, Nepal, Zanskar, and Mongolia over twenty years, which evince a diaphanous beauty that, to use a Homeric image, is "as soft as a hand of mist"; and an exceptional musician and singer-songwriter who plays piano and guitar—he also played the cornet in the film *The Cotton Club*— and over several months in 1994 was a guest guitarist with Van Morrison. Moments of his improvised piano playing can be seen and heard in many films, including *Pretty Woman* and *Time Out of Mind*, and he sang (and tap-danced) the part of Billy Flynn in the film *Chicago*. Since 2015, on an almost daily basis, he has been composing and recording on his iPhone luminous songs on which he plays both piano and guitar that are a kind of personal musical diary which, I hope, may eventually see the light of day.

A Buddhist practitioner for nearly fifty years, he has been an unwavering advocate for the homeless, for refugees, and for human rights in Tibet and around the world. He is also the founder of the Gere Foundation, which, among other things, is dedicated to the cultural preservation of Tibet and the Tibetan people, and whose foundation motto is by the eighth-century Indian Buddhist monk Shantideva—a motto that epitomizes Richard Gere's raison d'être: "All the suffering in the world arises out of wanting happiness for self. All happiness in the world arises out of wanting happiness for others."

When I began working on my book, I was hoping to talk to Richard about "Strawberry Fields Forever" and "Penny Lane" from both a musical and a Buddhist perspective. He generously agreed to do so, and we spoke for five hours at his home in the summer of 2022.

"I thought we'd start our conversation," I said to Richard, "by discussing 'Strawberry Fields Forever.' Three months after recording their album *Revolver* in the spring of 1966," I said, "the Beatles took a break from each other. John went to Almería, Spain, to act in the film *How I Won the War,* for which he had to get rid of his moptop and wear wire-rimmed granny glasses, and during the six weeks he was there he began to write 'Strawberry Fields.' It was the first time he'd been apart from the others, although Ringo came down at the end of John's stay, and John described his time there as a period of 'withdrawal' and began to feel that it was 'getting hard to be someone' and wasn't certain that it was going to 'all work out.' He seemed to be undergoing a kind of identity crisis at the age of twenty-six."

"Well, he was growing up," Richard observed. "He was still a young man trying to figure it out. Men generally mature much later than women; they don't usually become men until they're in their late thirties. But he's also Everyman: all men—and women—go through this kind of crisis of who am I? What am I? What am I going to do with myself? Am I the person I thought I was as a teenager or twenty-year-old? What's the point? What's real? What's real?"

"Nothing is real," I declared.

"Well, we're going to talk about that," Richard said.

"But John was not only an Everyman, he was also a Nowhere Man," I added.

"Right, that's what I mean. We're all Nowhere Men and Women. We don't bless ourselves into magnificence, we don't have the courage to do that, or find out *how* to do that, so we're kind of diminished, impoverished, in our worlds and our visions of possibility. That's probably why John was able to communicate with tens of millions of people. Whatever psychologically he was going through at that time was recognizable and spoke to all of us listening to that music. It wasn't some kind of alien experience that was coming from those records. And each one of the Beatles was communicating with and influencing all those millions of people; I'm sure you can find specifics of what all of those guys were going through, but I think that what made them, even today, so universally accepted and moving to us is that they were telling a universal story and not just the Beatles' story. It was and is our story as well, and will continue to be."

"What are your impressions of 'Strawberry Fields Forever?'" I asked him.

"What always struck me," Richard responded, "is that you can't separate the lyrics from the music. The words have meaning, but it's the interplay between the words and the music that gives us the narrative and produces the emotional reaction. And I've always been struck by how the music goes to a dark place when he sings 'Nothing is real.' It's dark, foreboding, threatening—he sings a minor melodic line that is unresolved, and then says '. . . and nothing to get hung about,' which all of a sudden becomes a major chord. And John's association of 'nothing is real' with darkness is interesting to me. At this point in *my* life, 'nothing is real' is a liberating experience, not a dark one, but for him it was, and you can hear that in the way the music expresses itself. The added-on orchestration with the dark coloration of cellos and trumpets deepens our experience of it."

"Regarding 'nothing is real,' I wanted to ask you if you could explain what the Buddha meant when he said: 'Everything is real and not real. Both real and not real. Neither real nor not real.' What does that mean?"

"The Buddha was saying that the concepts that we impose on reality are what limit us. All of those things are conceptual points of view—it's not this, it's not that, it's not the reification of this, it's not the negation of that—it's none of those things because in each one of those points of view you get caught in a dualistic conceptual trap. Things exist and they don't exist at the same time. They have a nominal existence that is unsupported by anything truly 'real.'"

"So when John says 'nothing is real,' how does this relate to what you're saying?"

"The Buddha spoke about the Two Truths, by which he meant 'absolute' and 'relative' truth. From the absolute truth point of view, 'reality' is all subjective experience, like a dream. A reflection. A mirage. There's nothing truly there. But that doesn't mean that it doesn't exist, it just doesn't exist the way it *appears* to exist. There's an *experience*, but it doesn't mean that it's real or true, any more than in a movie—it's not real, it's just light being filtered through celluloid and projected onto a screen, or now it's video or other electronic media. It gives the illusion of reality, there's something happening, there's an experience, we feel emotion. But when you deeply look at it, it's completely empty of solid reality. And the Buddha said that because it's empty, it *can* exist, it *can* come and go, it *can* manifest and then go away. It can change. But it's a projection of mind onto the screen of mind. Mind itself is the creator, even of itself, but it's this absolute mind that is ungraspable from any kind of conceptual reference point. From the absolute point of view there are no restrictions, no boundaries, no center, no meaning. Emptiness is the supreme birth vehicle of everything, and everything is open and possible. The same applies to the idea of self. Because the self is empty of inherent existence, it can come into existence, it can continually change, which it does, and then it can go away. And to me, John is playing with these things in 'Strawberry Fields.' He's saying, 'What's real? Am I real? Nothing is real. *I'm* not real, I think.'"

"John," I told Richard, "once said: 'I'm not interested in writing third-party songs. I like to write about *me* because I know me.' But in 'Strawberry Fields' he doesn't seem to really know who he is. Just look at the lines:

> Always, no sometimes, think it's me
> But you know I know when it's a dream
> I think, I know, I mean a 'Yes'
> But it's all wrong
> That is I think I disagree

There are six 'I's and three 'knows' here."

"Certainly John knows what he knows," Richard responded, "and he uses that as a starting and reference point, but he's looking for his true self. Every artist is probably looking for himself or herself. It's not necessarily going to be in that song or lyric or poem, but if it's courageous and good, it carries you deeper into knowing and feeling and clarity, whatever that may be.

"John's trying to discover the 'me' before the 'John.' So when he made that statement about how 'I like to write about me because I know me,' I think he meant: 'I know me but not in the full and absolute sense of I know me, I just use the labeled "me," and my experiences and emotions, just like an actor does, as a springboard. It's the fertile ground that things come out of.' As an actor, I don't work through *you,* I can't use somebody else's emotions and experiences. I use what of me that is analogous to a character I'm playing. All of us are trying to figure out who we are. It's the ultimate reason for being, and you hopefully find something that's much larger than what we've ever imagined."

"Don't you think," I asked, "that in this song John is also describing a kind of disintegrating self?"

"We all have countless voices inside our consciousness that are talking to us on different levels," Richard responded. "I happen to like this section of the song a lot because it's so naked in the way it depicts the unsurety, the slippery slope of everything, but I think it's more accurate to say that at this moment John is aware of his conceptual *bouncing*—'I think I'm right, no, I don't know, I think I know, one side of me says I'm full of shit, and the other side says, no you're not, well, you're only partly full of shit, no, you're completely wrong, no, actually I'm *right* . . . but I don't know, I was sure but now I'm not so sure, I'm trying, I'm doing the best I can to work my way through this.' There's a humility in that, and you can feel the echoes bouncing around the hard walls of his sense of self, which, from a Buddhist point of view, is something you have to soften, in order to damage the habitual belief that the self exists the way it *appears* to exist. You try to soften that so that other possibilities that are much vaster have the space to manifest. Ultimately, the only way to get to the metaphoric Strawberry Fields is to soften the distorted idea of a self. The degree with which we're hard and fast in our belief in the self—or a lack of it—is the deciding point on whether or not we're going to be liberated. Liberated literally from the causes of our suffering and from the impediments to us being happy, whether it's small case happy or large case Happy, which is complete liberation. And clearly John is playing with these ideas.

"The Dalai Lama often talked about the time when he visited an orthodox monastery—I think it was in Greece—and there was one monk who had been in solitary retreat for years and years. The monk came down to meet him, and the Dalai Lama asked him what he had been meditating on, and the monk simply said one word: Love. And His Holiness was so impressed and moved by that. The only way you can truly love is to soften and transform the idea of the self, otherwise it's just, What can I get out of this? What's in it for me? And it's defiled. But the great and the wise have always damaged this hard and heavy idea of the self.

"Now, this level of pure awareness can be characterized as love, and it doesn't lack emotion, but it's the purified aspect of human emotion at its highest—it's love but it's actually far beyond our normal love. The Buddhists would call it *bodhicitta*—the awakening mind. Love saturated with altruistic intention and the wisdom-energy to activate it. John talks about living with 'eyes closed,' but the awakened panoramic aspect of mind is innate to that pure level of awareness. In Buddhist teaching there's a lot of play with the idea of sleep or eyes closed and awakening. In fact, blindfolds are used in initiation rituals. You don't literally put the blindfold over your eyes, you put it over your forehead in a symbolic way, and then you ritually remove it and you're awake. You see for the first time, fresh, clean, pure, like a child."

"That reminds me," I said, "of something that the Yaqui shaman Don Juan declared to the anthropologist Carlos Castaneda: 'When you *see*, there are no longer familiar features in the world. Everything is new. Everything has never happened before. The world is incredible.'"

"He sounds like most of my teachers." [*Laughing*]

"When you spoke about the monk who was meditating on the word *love*," I reminded Richard, "I immediately thought about John Lennon himself who was continually singing about love. He thought that it was all you needed. In 'Across the Universe,' he sang about 'Limitless undying love which shines around me like a million suns / It calls me on and on across the universe,' and in 'The Word' he tells us that all we needed to do was to say the Word and we'd be free and would be like him, and of course the word was *Love*. John was forced to attend Sunday school when he was a kid, and he must have known about the Gospel of John—'In the beginning was the Word.' And in 'The Word' John sings: 'In the beginning I misunderstood / But now I've got it, the word is good.' John wasn't a big booster of God, but to me 'The Word' is the Gospel of John Lennon. He was really a lay apostle of love."

"I agree with you," Richard said. "It can sometimes look very twee and childish and silly on the page, but John certainly knew what vast, selfless love was like. I should tell you that I was very fortunate to have been in the presence of the Dalai Lama at a Catholic seminary outside of London many years ago, and he gave a talk there on the words of Jesus Christ. It was if you had never really heard the words before."

"You mean Jesus's words?"

"Yes. Forgiveness. Love your neighbor. Turn the other cheek. Selfless-ness. John was obviously taken by that. And for personal reasons, I'm sure. The fortunate among us have felt that kind of love with our mothers, a kind of total acceptance where you don't have to prove or earn it. It's just there."

"But John felt rejected by his mother," I said. "As he sang: 'Mother, you had me / But I never had you.'"

"Sure. We all feel that way to some degree. There are problems and blockages and emotional triggers. But I think that creative people know how to use these especially dark and mysterious emotions. John was very brave and naked in the way he did it."

"The psychoanalyst Wilfred Bion," I mentioned, "believed that in-stead of searching for illumination where the light shines the brightest, one should rather search for illumination and insight within the heart of darkness, and Bion declared that when one conducts an analysis, 'one must cast a *beam of intense darkness* so that something that has hitherto been obscured by the glare of illumination can glitter all the more in the darkness.'"

"But why does he talk about the darkness of it?" Richard asked. "I would say that the *light* of the unknown is where real insight comes from."

"You mean the lightness of unknowing?"

"Well, of course! The light at the center of the darkness. Unknowing doesn't put you in a dark, constricted place, unknowing is the great re-lease. Unknowing is the victory."

"But John is in fact going into the song's darkness," I pointed out. "It's like the poem by Mark Strand called 'Darker' in which the poet tells us that he has a key and opens the door and walks in, and then he writes: 'It is dark, and I walk in. / It is darker, and I walk in.'"

"Yes," Richard said, "John's not taking you back, he's taking you down, that's the choice he makes. He wasn't happy to just go *back* to memory lane. He wants to take you down to a darker place, and the music goes darker too—dark chords, dark cellos—it's not ethereal violins or like the piccolo trumpet at the end of 'Penny Lane.' He chooses to go into the unknown, which is 'What am I? Who am I?' That's the scariest place you can go. He's feeling insecure about the seeming surety of the fabric of reality, and it's getting hard to be John Lennon, to be anyone, and really believe in it. And then the question is, Is this just a dream?"

"Do you think that he might be having a lucid dream, that he knows he's dreaming in his dream? The German poet Novalis wrote: 'When you dream that you are dreaming, you are about to wake up.'"

"From a Buddhist point of view, sure, and for a yogi that's a powerful place to be such that you're completely lucid and aware in the dream. And of course you'd use that same ability in waking life to know that you're in the dream of *waking life*, seeing what we consider to be real as a spectacle. As my teachers assure me, 'Not a dream, but *like* a dream.'"

"In Dante's *Purgatorio*," I said, "Dante's pilgrim attempts to hug an empty shade, forgetting that it's not a human body. The spirit smiles and takes a step back from the pilgrim, and when the pilgrim begins to step forward again, the spirit pushes him back again and says—in the beautiful translation of Mary Jo Bang—'He gently told me I should let it go.' But on the other hand," I pointed out, "John says that he *knows* when it's a dream."

"But I'm not sure that he's aware enough of that," Richard said. "It's more like 'I don't know, I think, sometimes, maybe.' Knowing it's a dream is perhaps something that he aspires to, but it's not easy, it's something one has to really work at over many lifetimes. I think that he latches onto something and second-guesses himself, but the through line here is basically 'Nothing is real.'

"But then he resolves it. He's decided to touch the darkness, which for most people is deeply scary, but there's a courage that's empowering this. It's like the line in Bob Dylan's song 'Forever Young' that goes: 'May you build a ladder to the stars / And climb on every rung.' That to me is the best line in the song—'Climb on *every* rung'—you can't skip a rung, you've got to do every rung on the way or you'll have to go back and do it again anyhow, otherwise it's always going to be there as an impediment. And John is obviously courageous in his willingness to go there. To question himself. It's as if he's saying, 'I'm not sure what I'm going to reach down there, it's scary to let go, but nothing to get hung about, I don't know, it's okay, oh no, I'm going to let go, Strawberry Fields Forever, okay, I'm going to hold on to that, that's safe ground, but in the end you have to let it go of even Strawberry Fields."

"I was wondering, Richard, if you've ever envisioned your own personal idea of Strawberry Fields."

"Yeah, I guess I'm looking for my version of Strawberry Fields. Freedom, openness, no hope or fear, saturated with love. With kindness. In Buddhist terms it's called *rigpa*, the recognition of pure awareness with no subject or object to cling to. No narrative. No opinions, no choices, no decision making, no labels, it's just awareness—it's not a *me* that is aware of being aware, it's just awareness itself, and it's this pure, wide open, unreferenced point of awareness—mind essence, which in terms of language is about as close as you can get to God. So that would be the pinnacle, the mountain peak of the idea of a beautiful place to me, but in that realm there's not even a difference between beautiful and ugly, good and bad, up and down. So my idea of Strawberry Fields wouldn't be literal, it would just be freedom. Clarity. Knowing. Being liberated from concepts that constrict me from the vast openness of love. But still I long for the here-and-now love in my wife's eyes, my children's laughter, childhood memories of summers on Cayuga Lake with my family, the kindness of my teachers, my father singing the old songs."

"In his song 'God' from his album *John Lennon / Plastic Ono Band*," I said, "John goes about smashing idols, declaring that he doesn't believe in Tarot, in yoga, in Jesus, in Kennedy, in Elvis, in Buddha, in Beatles. In the light of what you were just saying about constricting concepts, it sounds to me as if he's trying to rid himself of a lot of conceptual baggage. And in a similar vein, I'm also reminded of the Buddhist monk Linji Yixuan's famous statement: 'If you meet the Buddha on the road, kill him.'"

"Surely, the Buddha didn't believe in Buddha either," Richard replied [*laughing*].

"I've been told that in Buddhism, one speaks about the clear light nature of mind. Does this have something to do with *rigpa*?"

"Yes, that's *rigpa*. Actually it's the *recognition* of the clear light nature of mind. Not strawberries or strawberry fields that go on forever. It's freedom, it's not just another heavenly realm where everything's okay and nice and like a picnic or a little vacation. If it just means a pleasure place where you're on a vacation in samsara and where nobody's going to hassle or hurt you and where there's nothing to get hung about, it doesn't mean you've been released from samsara [the endless cycle of birth, death, and rebirth]. Peace and happiness isn't the goal. It's pretty good, but you can get stuck there because it feels so good. That's not liberation. It's not bad but it's not the ultimate thing.

"Strawberries rot if you don't eat them, and fields go through different seasons, so it's a kind of childish notion that it will always be there forever. It's a child's view of the universe. In the nature of reality *nothing* can last forever, other than the clear light nature of mind itself, which is of a completely different order of experience than happiness or unhappiness. And sure, you'd rather be in a happy dream than one that scares us or one that makes us literally suffer or have the experience of suffering. But happiness and unhappiness are both projections of mind."

"When I first interviewed John Lennon," I told Richard, "he said to me: 'Strawberry Fields is anywhere you want to go.'"

"But of course Strawberry Fields is a place you can go to," Richard said. "It's a state of mind. I don't think that John literally thinks, Oh, if only I could, I'd get a ticket and get on a train and go to Strawberry Fields. But, sure, he wants to go back to the Strawberry Field orphanage grounds where things weren't so complicated and where he had fun playing with his friends.

"Many children have a cherished playroom or a special tree or whatever. For me, when I was young, I experienced that kind of Strawberry

Fields lying in my backyard at night, my back on the ground, feeling the solidness of the earth, and smelling the wet grass around me, and looking up at the stars. And I didn't find that dark, I found that the night was dark, but I found it filled with light and possibility. John was playing with his friends in Strawberry Field, and I was lying in my suburban backyard looking up at the stars.

"But it's not like that's the end—it's just the merest taste of the vastness. It's not ultimately going to take you to clear light. As an analogy, yes. But the way out of suffering is to abandon all conceptual thinking, the conceptual part of the brain that says, 'I want Strawberry Fields but I don't want hell,' because this presupposes that there's a Strawberry Fields and that there's a hell, but it doesn't acknowledge that the mind itself is making both Strawberry Fields *and* hell. The real liberation, we're told, is when you realize that there's no difference between Strawberry Fields and hell. It's the conceptualizing itself that's holding us back from our innate magnificence.

"I think that John is trying to work toward that understanding and to find out what layers he has to go through to get there. He's going down and back into his memory, back down into stuff that was difficult, and Strawberry Field was the one place where he felt good. So there's a twenty-six-year-old John Lennon who's going with his memory and emotional self down *and* back—he's acknowledging both—and is sharing it with us."

"Perhaps," I suggested, "you could think of the real Strawberry Fields as a Buddha Field."

"You could, but that Buddha Field isn't really a mental or sensory experience. It's the underlying emptiness that that experience would come out of. And ultimately the only way to get to that Strawberry Fields is to transform the idea of a solid, eternal self. It's the only way."

"Speaking of concepts," I told Richard, "the fourth-century Christian bishop Gregory of Nyssa once said something quite remarkable. 'Concepts,' he declared, 'create idols; only wonder can grasp anything.'"

"I love that," Richard said. "The wonder that's the embrace of mystery. The not-knowing. Some people mistrust the mystery, but I choose to think that we're all participants in an adventure of mysteries. Mirrors within mirrors within mirrors. It's a spectacle, and it's okay for it to be a spectacle, but it's the *attachment* to any part of that emerging and creative spectacle that gives us hope and fear: 'Can I hold on to that—I'm fearful that I can't.' So because of the way humans are constituted and the way our brains associate, we live in snapshots. We take a snapshot of the illusion of us right now, and then that lingers because it has an afterlife. An afterglow. We don't continually take new snapshots as everything is changing—sometimes slowly, sometimes quickly—although everything is in a state of breaking down and changing. We live within a snapshot as long as we possibly can, and then circumstances become so dramatic that we realize we're in a different place now. So we have a new snapshot, and then we live in *that* snapshot for a while, so we're never really directly in reality, we're living in a snapshot of conceptual projecting mind, grasping onto the surface of things. But the Great Ones have let that go—there are no expectations, no making choices in the sense that we normally make choices, it's just being in flow, just being there with impeccable motivation and a sense of humor."

"The French film director Jean-Luc Godard famously declared: 'The cinema is truth twenty-four frames per second.'"

"The Tibetans would say it's more like 365 times per second! Apparently there are yogis who can be conscious of 365 separate events within a second. We're just kind of stuck ... floating in these isolated snapshots. Movies look so good because they're twenty-four-times-a-second where you get zapped with a new still—pom-pom-pom! You're being hit with that, and the brain is delighted."

"It feels like it's real," I said.

"Better than real," Richard told me. "But the video experience, which is a continuous flow, doesn't delight us. They take video and transform that into twenty-four frames a second so it can achieve that magical effect."

"'Roll away the reel world, the reel world, the reel world!' wrote James Joyce."

"I think," Richard commented, "that actors can be aware of the ephemeral nature of emotions because we make them, we conjure them, that's our job, we know they can be manufactured or coaxed into being. They appear to be real, but the world of the movie is conjured. Edited. Manipulated. It's not unfolding as it is; it was constructed in pieces. We're just not aware of it. The same in our normal waking life—we're constructing it just the same way an actor, an editor, and a director are constructing a movie experience. So all of this conceptuality, these narratives, these movies become a playground, a spectacle. It's a playground, a spectacle, it's the mind playing with itself. Entertaining itself is illusion.

"One of my teachers, Nyoshul Khen Rinpoche, once told me: 'I have friends who like to watch movies and TV and go to plays,' and he added, 'I don't really understand that—I just watch my mind. What a spectacle!' So at Rinpoche's level there's no attachment to it. You watch the spectacle of the universe doing its dance, its movie projection . . . one movie after another. Endlessly."

"The film and theater director Elia Kazan," I said, "wrote a manifesto that he called 'The Actor's Vow,' which is an exhortation to encourage actors to take their rightful place onstage and to be themselves. And Kazan encourages them to open their hearts and throats, to be vulnerable, to admit rejection, pain, shame, and frustration, and, most importantly, to reveal the parts of themselves they have hidden from the world. And the vow concludes 'I will work on it. I will raise my voice, I will be heard.'"

"It's wonderful, I love that," Richard said. "The vow is for courage. When someone is holding back and constricted, you can hear it in the voice. So Kazan is saying you've got to be brave because you've got nothing to lose. You have to be yourself and be confident and not care what anyone else thinks. But in my opinion what he doesn't have in there is a kind of humble commitment to do what you're doing as a gift, an offering."

"A gift to whom?"

"To whomever we're engaging. To whoever is witnessing. To the universe. I'm not doing this to enrich or codify the self, I'm going to do this opening up because there's some good stuff that's going to come out of this, and I'm offering it. Reifying and protecting the self doesn't take you to a good place. But the motivation that is ultimately going to be of value is to offer yourself from the best place you can, and trust it's of value in the world. Not because it's going to make you famous or rich or loved, but so that you become a vehicle to bring love and understanding into the world. It's actually going to be diminishing the distorted part of the self. We all have to function in the waking dream of this world with generosity, with love, with kindness, and responsibility. You can do all of those things, even in a dream. But that's the only thing that I see missing in that wonderful vow."

"Do you think that John Lennon fulfilled this vow?"

"Well, I think any artist would want to come from that place. You want to show up, you get one time around in this body that's always changing, and you go through a challenging process, and then you get another shot in another body that's also always changing. The dividing point of what I think is a successful life is acknowledging who you are and committing that voyage as a gift to your community and to the universe. But the voyage isn't to enrich the idea of *you*, it's to enrich the idea of those levels of mind that are purely generous and selfless. The ritual commitment of the work is: I'm going to do this for the welfare of all sentient beings, and this releases and frees you from the damaging aspects of the distorted self. And I think that John was definitely playing with that idea a lot."

"He seemed to have that effect on people," I said.

"And he had that effect because it was really him. I have no doubt that he was a complicated guy, and it wasn't all Strawberry Fields and flowers. He was courageous and able to show the good and also the bad and the dark stuff, and he kept at it, but I'm sure it was a bumpy road."

"But Paul McCartney has also given a great gift to people."

"Certainly. I think Paul is completely himself. I was mesmerized and surprised and delighted to see the Paul in Peter Jackson's *Get Back* documentary. He's supertalented and awesome and deep and terrific. A true leader. He could do everything. And the songs just come out of him! Even John was blown away that Paul could come up with five songs a day, whereas he struggled—maybe one song a month, he didn't have extras, everything that he had ended up on the records. But Paul was flowing with them like water from a spring, a constant flow. Beautiful melodies and words and quirky chord changes. He heard the arrangements very clearly in his head, but at the same time it's not an in-your-face kind of creativity like John's. In fact, I think Paul is probably more pure in his humility, frankly, and I think that like John he really wants the world to be a better place. I would never question the authenticity of where he's coming from.

"Grotowski [the Polish theater director Jerzy Grotowski] believed that an actor's job is to find that one character they most intimately embody, and that should essentially be the character they play in everything. Of course, an actor can play a wide variety of roles, but which is that one defining character that they have real power playing? The one essential, mythic hero that their life force in this lifetime most closely represents."

"Do you think that each of the Beatles found that character for himself?"

"When the Beatles were starting to come apart and each one went off on his own," Richard said, "I think that George found his essential mythic character. And the essential things that John and Paul already were started to come out even more."

"And what about Ringo?" I asked.

"Well, Ringo seems to have been himself right from the beginning!" [*Laughing*] But if you take these four guys together, they somehow make up one person, one entity."

"When the Beatles were recording 'Strawberry Fields,'" I recalled, "John told the producer George Martin that he wanted the sound of the song to be 'heavier.' But when they were working on 'Penny Lane,' Paul said that he wanted that song to have 'a clean American sound,' and after you've listened to the 'Strawberry Fields Forever' side of the 45 single and turn it over, you're in a radically different sonic realm."

"Yes," Richard agreed, "you get the feeling that you're looking up at blue skies. I think it's a brilliant song, and I like it better all the time. Do you know the painting called *The Street* by Balthus [the Polish French twentieth-century artist]? It shows a town square, and all of these people are on the street doing all kinds of different things. [A cook strolls on the sidewalk, a carpenter carries a plank across the street, a girl plays with a racquet and ball, a mother in an apron carries a child in a sailor suit, and a boy walks stiffly like a bandleader.] They're like vignettes, and it somehow reminds me of the mood of 'Penny Lane.'

"And when I listen to that song I'm getting the feeling of Paul sitting on a park bench, and it's a beautiful day, his eyes are seeing things and his mind is drifting, and life is being filtered like light through the trees, there's nothing to get hung about, there's a comfort level of being just fine watching the spectacle. He doesn't have to go to a dark place. Some things are strange, but that's okay. A barber is showing photographs of his customers, a pretty nurse is selling poppies, a fireman's holding an hourglass and then rushes into the barber's from the pouring rain. But up until then there's been a clear blue suburban sky. It's kind of like a daydream."

"William Wordsworth," I said, "talks about 'the everyday sublime.' The Cuban novelist Alejo Carpentier refers to 'the marvelous real.' A student asks a Buddhist teacher, 'What is the Way?' and the teacher replies: 'Ordinary Mind is the Way.' And the Japanese Rinzai monk Sokei-an wrote: 'He who truly attains awakening knows that deliverance is to be found right where he is. He lives his daily life in awakened awareness. His every act from morning to night is his religion.' 'Penny Lane' seems to me to be a kind of Buddhist song."

"It's like a Zen koan," Richard suggested. "'How can you achieve enlightenment driving your car?' And the answer is: 'By driving your car.' If you're actually driving your car in awareness that's pretty close to what we're talking about here."

"Keeping your eye on the road."

"Yes, you're in the world, a world that you've ultimately created. This movie out here that I seem to be walking through is my movie that I'm writing and directing. We walk through the world that we think belongs to the world and that exists without us, and we think that if we remove ourselves the world is still there—but that's impossible."

"What?"

"I know," Richard said, laughing. "We've talked about this before, and I know that you can't go there."

"I believe that if that proverbial tree falls in the forest it makes a sound, even if I'm not there to hear it."

"I know you do because you're a materialist. You believe that it exists from its own side without you." [*Laughing*]

"But I also believe in subtle energies and mind-to-mind communication," I declared, "and in any case I'm certainly not materialistic!" [*Laughing*]

"But from my point of view *all* of this is just a projection of 'me'— whatever me is. This doesn't exist without me. You are my dream. My experience of you is my dream. What I take from you, I put it out there, you're in the mirror. There's a mirror reflecting back to me, and it's a feedback loop. None of the experience of 'out there' exists without a consciousness engaging it."

"What you're saying really reminds me of that brilliant passage in *Alice's Adventures in Wonderland* when Tweedledee and Tweedledum are conversing with Alice, and I can't help quoting it to you."

"The Red King's dreaming now," said Tweedledee, "and what do you think he's dreaming about?"

Alice said, "Nobody can guess that."

"Why, about *you*!" Tweedledee exclaimed, clapping his hands triumphantly. "And if he left off dreaming about you, where do you suppose you'd be?"

"Where I am now, of course," said Alice.

"Not you!" Tweedledee retorted contemptuously. "You'd be nowhere. Why, you're only a sort of thing in his dream!"

"If that there King was to wake," added Tweedledum, "you'd go out—bang!—just like a candle!"

"I shouldn't!" Alice exclaimed indignantly. "Besides, if *I'm* only a thing in his dream, what are *you,* I should like to know?"

"Ditto," said Tweedledum.

"Ditto, ditto," cried Tweedledee.

"So please don't wake up, Richard, because I have some more questions to ask you [*laughing*]. But while I'm still here—unless you think otherwise!—I wanted to ask you about the way John and Paul view the spectacle of life."

"John's *looking* for Strawberry Fields," Richard told me. "Paul is *in* Penny Lane."

"It's in his ears and in his eyes."

"He's there, and he's seeing the simple beauty of the spectacle of life. The utter ordinariness of the mystery. Again, there's a great humility in this, and a sense of equality. None of these experiences Paul talks about here are good or bad, no 'this one's better than that.' He's not complaining, he's not making judgments, he just has a sense of the delight of the world."

"The French anthropologist Claude Lévi-Strauss remarked that 'the secret of the world is hidden in the world.'"

"And I feel the same way," Richard concurred. "You know those hidden pockets in New York City where you can sit on a bench and hopefully you're under a tree and everyone's outside and things and people are moving—that one is having a drama, this one is walking a dog, that person is kissing another person, this one is crying, that one has an ice cream cone. It's the delight of the spectacle of life. To appreciate the life force as it's moving through awareness without judging it—Paul's only comment on it is 'very strange.' He doesn't say, That scares me, or I want to change that and make it less strange. And then there are those beautiful lines:

> Behind the shelter in the middle of a roundabout
> A pretty nurse is selling poppies from a tray
> And though she feels as if she's in a play
> She is anyway

She's in the spectacle, but whatever she thinks conceptually about it, she is anyway. It's a deep observation and reveals a deep understanding and acceptance of his observations. She's aware that she's in a nurse's uniform—a costume—with poppies on a tray, and you iris out and see that the whole thing is a play. It's like that Balthus painting of walking, strolling, strutting people. It's this proscenium that's being projected. This idea of being in a play. It's like Paul's got a notebook out and he's just sitting there and watching all this stuff, and it's a play, just like in the Balthus painting. It's a play of movement and personality, and he's watching it. He doesn't say it's bad, he doesn't say I don't want it to happen. It's just a bit odd. How bizarre. What a spectacle! And I get a great source of comfort from this song—you don't have to push the river, it's okay, just jump in the stream. It's alright. And it's a very accepting point of view for sure. Whereas John struggles a lot."

"Well, Richard," I said, giving up, "at least you've got Shakespeare on your side, and the Bard seems to agree with you. At the conclusion of *A Midsummer Night's Dream,* Puck turns to the audience and says:

> If we shadows have offended,
> Think but this, and all is mended,
> That you have but slumbered here
> While these visions did appear.
> And this weak and idle theme,
> No more yielding but a dream.

"Shakespeare was a great yogi," Richard concurred. "But while we're in the dream, we behave within it as if it's real. Even knowing we're dreaming we act as if we're not . . . as if it still matters."

"The strangest and to me the most dreamlike image in 'Penny Lane,'" I mentioned to Richard, "is that of the fireman with his hourglass. And apparently the image of the hourglass was John's contribution to the song."

"In the context of our discussion," Richard said, "you might see the fireman as a bodhisattva [a person who is able to enter nirvana but delays doing so out of compassion in order to help others attain enlightenment] who's putting out fires and removing suffering from all beings. And he's got an hourglass so he's only got a finite amount of time to be able to do it.

"Universes have a dynamic such that they're born and grow, then retreat and return to what has been translated as a single space particle, and the dynamic potential of that particle again emerges in a big bang as a newly manifesting universe which expands in detail and size and vastness, and then it reaches an equilibrium point when it can't get more vast, and it starts to compress back to that single particle. So maybe that hourglass is a world system."

"And then you turn over the hourglass."

"Right, you turn it, and whoom!, world system over. And a new world system emerges from that single particle, and then back to the single particle again. And the bodhisattva has committed to being in world system after world system after world system."

"So in this world system the fireman with his hourglass turns out to be the bodhisattva of Penny Lane!"

"Well, you got me started on this," Richard said, laughing. "And we could go on and on!"

LAURIE ANDERSON

For one cycle of creation, Shiva dances. For the next cycle
he dreams. We think we are living in the real world and
Shiva is dancing. We are not. He is dreaming.
  —quoted by Kenneth Rexroth in *Classics Revisited*

A critic once understatedly remarked that Laurie Anderson "excels in
different forms of expression." She is, among other things, a musician, a
composer, a singer-songwriter, an author, a poet, a painter, a sculptor, a film-
maker, a performance and video artist, an inventor of musical instruments,
and an electronic music pioneer. "I used to define myself as a multimedia
artist," she told an interviewer, "but that's so clumsy. Put a gun to my head
and I say, I tell stories, and sometimes they look like paintings, sometimes
they look like songs, sometimes they look like films. They're just stories."

The anthropologist and cyberneticist Gregory Bateson recounted the
following: "There was once a man who had a computer, and he asked it,
'Do you compute that you will ever be able to think like a human being?'
And after assorted grindings and beepings, a slip of paper came out of the
computer that said, 'That reminds me of a story.'" It is stories that make us
humans—"God created human beings," declared Rabbi Israel of Rishin,
"because He loved stories"—and as the psychologist James Hillman has
stated: "We all need to be re-storied in order to restory the imagination to
a primary place in consciousness in each of us, regardless of age."

Laurie Anderson is one of the great re-storyers of our time, and her stories have their roots in the subsoil of the dreams, reveries, and memories of her childhood. The French philosopher Gaston Bachelard remarked that "the seasons of memory are eternal because they are faithful to the colors of the first time," and he suggested that "an excess of childhood is the germ of a poem" ... and, one might add, of a song or a story as well. Laurie Anderson's stories have always been faithful to those colors, as have "Strawberry Fields Forever" and "Penny Lane," and she invited me to visit her in her Lower Manhattan studio in September 2022 to talk about them.

When we sat down, she told me: "What a treasure chest there is in those two songs," and over several hours she opened up the chest and disclosed and illuminated their treasures.

"I've been asking people how they envision Strawberry Fields," I said to Laurie, "and so I wanted to ask you that question as well."

"For me," she said, "Strawberry Fields was a place I used to dream about when I was about five years old. It was a dream island that was in fact based on a real island. Our family lived in Glen Ellyn, Illinois, next to a lake called Lake Ellyn, and in that lake there was a real island where I spent a lot of time as a kid. But my dream island was covered with thickets and brambles and berries—there were strawberries in there as well—and it had the secret-place-by-the-water feeling of *The Wind in the Willows* [the children's novel by Kenneth Grahame, which recounts the adventures of Mole, Ratty, Badger, and Mr. Toad]. There were secret brambly places that the animals liked, and as in *The Wind in the Willows* the animals in my dream island were all bachelors, and they had little cars and rowboats and tea sets, and they wore raccoon coats and wrote letters to each other and shared messages and had secret meetings and spring-cleaned and did all kinds of things. They were busy guys. And they had these special hideaways that I fantasized about when I was a child. And I really wanted to have my own hideaway just as they did.

"Anyway, when I first heard 'Strawberry Fields Forever,' which was in 1967 when I was attending Barnard College, I imagined it as that thicketed childhood place where one could play, and for children it's very important to have a wild place like that to play in. But most of all it was a magical place where anything could happen and you could just imagine things. You'd think, 'What if?' And there were a series of what ifs—'What if that cloud fell down right now? What if everything was purple?'—nothing seems etched in stone at that point of your life, everything seems a little bit arbitrary, so you'd stop asking 'Why is it like that?' and would instead start posing the question 'What if?'

"The idea of reality is something that's on kids' minds a lot—like, Are you really my mom? And then people would say, no that's just an imaginary question, so you had to start making categories of real and imaginary, and that's a big job for a little child's mind to do. The first lines in 'Strawberry Fields Forever' mention strawberries and reality, and those are the two things that made me feel that I understood the song, and it was those two elements that connected me to my childhood."

"In your case," I said, "the song was 'Let me take you down 'cos I'm going to Lake Ellyn.'"

"It *was* that," she responded, "it rang exactly like that, and it still takes me there in a second."

"When I once asked John Lennon what Strawberry Fields meant to him, he told me: 'Everywhere is somewhere, and Strawberry Fields is anywhere you want to go.'"

"That's it," Laurie said. "It's consciousness. It's your mind. It's your mind forever. Consciousness forever. Lake Ellyn forever. And on top of that it's imagination and it's freedom. Absolute freedom."

"Strawberry Fields is an image," I said, "and James Hillman declared that 'images are where the psyche is' and urged us to 'engage the image' and let it express itself in its own language. And the writer Elias Canetti admonished: 'You have neglected the images. Addicted to affirmations, you failed to take time for images. Have they become extinguished, did they fall asleep, did they disintegrate?' Which is to say that we diminish our lives when we lose touch with the images that sustain them."

"It's because we often put them into words right away," Laurie responded. "I think that's at least part of it. Putting them into words is an extremely tricky thing. And I've become particularly aware of this with the work I've recently been doing with this crazy image-to-text program."

"What program is that?" I asked.

"There's a place called the Australian Institute for Machine Learning, which is part of the University of Adelaide, and it has a language supercomputer that works with algorithms of people's writings."

"How did you find out about it?"

"They contacted me a couple of years ago and asked me if I would like to work with it. So I asked what it does, and they said that it makes a database with everything a person has written and published and puts it into an AI program and then tries to make sentences out of those lines. For example, it might take all of Shakespeare's plays and poetry, and by using models of comparison or similarities, it can create language remixes. In a way, it's like a kind of William Burroughs cutup, but instead of doing it with scissors, it does it through algorithms.

"In my case, they put everything I've ever written, recorded, and published into the supercomputer, and when you feed it a few key words, it uses these algorithms to compose sentences. But half of them will be in 'monkeys with typewriter' style. They don't make any sense. They're gibberish. Twenty percent of it is kind of interesting, and the rest is really interesting. It makes logical and stylistic jumps that I wouldn't normally make with my own rules of how a sentence should go or how a mind usually thinks about things or how categories usually operate.

"So if you, Jonathan, put everything you've ever written into this supercomputer, and then you feed it a few key words, it would use all of your associations to come up with unexpected sentences. It's like you're collaborating with a gigantic version of your own brain. You'll recognize some of the associations that it's trying to make. AI is looking for meaning—it's a meaning machine, just as we humans are meaning machines. We're looking for it everywhere and sometimes we find it in meaningless words or if we say something like Oohoowareyooooou? Suddenly this word has a lot of meaning if it's said in a certain way, like the way a mother would say words to a baby. It's baby-talk but it's full of meaning, it's full of love."

"It's the music of the words," I suggested.

"Yes, it's the music of the words, and that's the meaning."

"With regard to words and music," I said, "I wanted to quote you something that Herman Melville once wrote: 'Where the deepest word ends, there music begins with its supersensuous and all-confounding intimacies.' I'm quoting this because in your own work, words and music are so integrated. But do you sometimes find that at a certain point music needs to takes over?"

"What Melville says is a beautiful way to put it. And yes, absolutely, when you can't say it, sing it. But you can also do a lot of things with breath, you can say lots of words in many different ways. Like, say, the word **paper,** and then make it softer (paper) and then softer (*paper*). The hundreds of ways you can think about paper can be revealed in all those different tones of voice. And that, too, is music because it's *sounded* words, words made of sound. And so you have another universe to pick from, another universe that's all about emotion, the way you feel about something can be put in there. That's why soundtracks are so dangerous in films because they tell you how to feel about an image. Depending on the music, this very same picture can make you feel nostalgic, scared, or happy. Images are more neutral, but once you put a sound to it, you're told how to feel."

"Getting back to what you were saying before about meaning," I said, "John Lennon begins his beautiful song 'Julia' by gently intoning the words 'Half of what I say is meaningless / But I say it just to reach you' with just one note."

"And in 'Strawberry Fields,'" Laurie pointed out, "it's almost impossible to understand what his words supposedly mean, and that's what I think that song is about as well, the meaninglessness of words—'No sometimes I think I know I mean a Yes it's all wrong I think I disagree.' Descartes said 'I think, therefore I am,' and John Lennon is splitting himself up into various little philosophical schools. Just because you think, are you there? I think, therefore I am? I am, therefore I think? Which one is it? It's as if in that song he's pouring all of his thoughts into something that sounds like conversation and debate, or even an argument, because the he doesn't understand the other side . . ."

"The other side of what?"

"His own brain. As he says: 'Misunderstanding all you see.' It's as if he's having a boxing match with himself, or it's like shadow puppetry. That song is really a kind of duet."

"Do you think you could try to put some lines from 'Strawberry Fields' and maybe from 'Penny Lane' into this lyric generator?"

"What lines should we try?"

"How about 'Let me take you down / 'Cos I'm going to Strawberry Fields / Nothing is real.'"

"Okay, but maybe it would be better to write 'because' instead of ''cos' because it might not recognize that [*laughing*]. So if you put something from 'Strawberry Fields' into the database of everything I've ever said, it will look for 'strawberries' and for 'fields' and for something 'real,' and it will try to compose sentences out of that, as well as some of the other words from the song. It will put them into another context, and this version will be different every single time. Let's try doing this a couple of times so that you can see how it works.

"Here's how the opening of the first one came out:

> There's nothing to it
> There'll be a time when I don't know who I am
> Look out for me in the fields, in the Fields
> Because I'm not here right now

Take me with you
We're going nowhere
But you can you feel me ebb and flow
Like a river full of gold and snow
You can see my real eyes in the back of my head So what I do I do
This is true
Come down and kiss me
Put your tongue in my mouth
Lie on my tongue
And let me taste you
Strawberry wafers on your lips . . .

"And now let's generate it again:

In the fields
In the Fields
This is me Strawberry
And Strawberry
It's you I'm talking to
But I don't know how to talk to you
Is there nothing you want to ask me, or can I just take things as
    they come
Because this is what I've been thinking of doing for a while now
I'm just going to say
I'm or I'm not I'm
Then I'm
Going to lie down
And go to sleep
And it will flow
Out of my head
You know
There are things in life that are real
Let me tell you about them

"The thing about this, sadly," Laurie confessed, "is that I could do this all day. If you said to me, Let's see what happens when you do twenty thousand more of these, I'd say, Great! Let's see what happens! I need to be stopped [*laughing*]."

"But before you stop, could you try doing this with some lines from 'Penny Lane'?"

"You choose," she said.

"Okay, how about 'And though she feels as if she's in a play / She is anyway.'"

"Here goes:

> She is a woman
> And I'm a man and
> We don't play
> That game, though
> What she feels in her heart, she's not
> Sure of anyway
> So let's try
> To get to the bottom of it by
> Making something out of nothing
> See if we can figure it out
> If not, what to do about it
> Well, as you know,
> I'm all for ideas and such
> But I don't believe that they're going to
> Get it right
> Or if they are, then there's nothing to be done
> As far as I know, no one knows where she is
> Or where she has been or where she might be

"And here's the opening part of the second one:

She says she feels
She doesn't know who I am, that this is a play
She's making it up as she goes along, that we
Are on different times and she's trying to get me
To talk to her but I don't seem to be able to talk at all
It's as if I can't hear what I want to say
As though I'm not even in the room right now.
And is there such a thing as being in the wrong place at the
    wrong time? . . .

"I could easily get hooked on this too," I admitted. "And it's so interesting to me that the question about 'Who am I?' appears in both the first 'Strawberry Fields' version ('There'll be a time when I don't know who I am') and the second 'Penny Lane' version ('She doesn't know who I am')."

"I love 'Who am I?' songs," Laurie told me.

"John Lennon," I said, "has a song called 'Look at Me,' and in it he asks the question 'Who am I?' and then sings 'Nobody knows but me / Nobody else can see / Just you and me.'"

"Nobody knows but me," Laurie repeated the line, "but it's also a mirror love song about someone understanding another person. It's like looking in the mirror and saying 'Who am I?' and it's like a song by Lou Reed called 'Who Am I? (Tripitena's Song)' which begins:

Sometimes I wonder who I am
The world seeming to pass me by
A younger man now getting old
I have to wonder what the rest of life will hold
I hold a mirror to my face
There are some lines that I could trace
To memories of loving you
A passion that breaks reason in two

"Both John's and Lou's songs are about reflections, they're looking in the mirror and asking a question, and asking the mirror or their lover to respond. It's a conversation about perception, it's looking at the self and standing back from it to see who that might be. And in 'Strawberry Fields' it's a man looking at an aspect of himself and realizing that he's a dream, that he's a series of stories that he's made up about himself. So if you can get back to this feeling of sensation without labeling all of that stuff—and of course one of the biggest goals of meditation is to stop labeling and just pay attention to how you feel—then you'll realize that the doors between realities are very thin. And when John says 'Let me take you down' he's not taking you down a notch, he's inviting you to go into a psychic space where nothing is real, where you start wondering whether that paisley tree is real."

"Paisley tree?"

"You know, all of the stuff you see when you do drugs, it all turns paisley, unfortunately. Paisley is *not* my favorite pattern. In fact, I'm allergic to paisley, I have to say."

"Remind me to ask you later what drug that was," I said, "because I'd like to pass on that one. But did things really appear paisley to you?"

"Yeah, they did. I guess that's what you see when you close your eyes. 'Living is easy with eyes closed.' You see hallucinatory things, and to me 'Strawberry Fields' is, in part, a psychedelic song about what you see when you try to see through our conventional idea of reality or all of the mundane stuff that we have here, before you realize that everything is illuminated and much stranger than you ever thought. And that's what I think John Lennon is saying. Things are a lot stranger than anything you've ever dreamed of."

"In 'Strawberry Fields,'" I mentioned, "John Lennon sings 'But you know I know when it's a dream.' I wonder if he might be referring to the idea of a lucid dream, becoming aware in your dream that you're dreaming. Have you ever had that experience?"

"Yes. It's not really usual but it's not unfamiliar, and it usually has something to do with dreaming about Lou. I'll be dreaming, and Lou might come into the room and I say, 'Where have you been?' And he says, 'Oh, I've been on another planet. Maybe you could come by sometime?' And then I know that this is a dream. But he might be dreaming it too, so I may be in his dream. I don't know, but we're meeting there somewhere. And somewhere where some people go to is back to their childhood. They go into a simpler place where they had more primal perceptions."

"The German poet Novalis," I said, "wrote: 'When we dream that we are dreaming, we are about to awaken.' Do you know what he means?"

"I think he means that dreaming is another state of consciousness, and then you go into the waking state, and that is just as much a dream state because you not only realize that the dream is lucid but you get a lucid feeling about life, which is really not so real either. And this quote gives you insight into that. 'Strawberry Fields' is about consciousness and reality and dream states, and when we begin to think about these things you realize that the ultimate dream state is death. And as Robert Thurman [the American Buddhist scholar, author, and translator] once said: 'There are no dead people.'"

"In his powerful song 'She Said She Said,'" I told Laurie, "which John Lennon wrote about six months before he went to Spain, he sings: 'She said I know what it's like to be dead / I know what it is to be sad / And she's making me feel like I've never been born.' Some people think that this mood might have carried over to his song 'Strawberry Fields Forever' and that for the first time he began to realize that he was no longer just 'John Lennon Beatle' and he became a bit confused and possibly depressed, and this song might be seen as a reflection of his state of mind."

"I'm not so sure about that," Laurie said. "Maybe 'Strawberry Fields' is a song about confusion. There's a difference between somebody who's caught in depression and someone who's making a big painting of an entire landscape, like Bosch or Brueghel. John Lennon is a painter, 'Strawberry Fields' is a painting, and although he's someone who's talking about being lost and who's embodying that feeling and is really feeling it, it's like what Mingyur Rinpoche [a renowned Tibetan teacher] said about feeling sad but not *being* sad. He said try to practice how to feel sad without actually being sad. And this is a wonderful distinction between feeling and being. And for me, that's one of the things that 'Strawberry Fields' is about—feeling but not being sad. It's John Lennon having this back-and-forth conversation. He's an artist who's making a *portrait* of confusion and argument and is presenting a lucid and clear description of that.

"You have to separate the 'I' in this song from the I that is the writer of the song. John's a songwriter, and it's exhilarating for him to get that description of confusion right. He's a beautiful painter and he's making a beautiful picture of that, and it's an act of creation to write a song about depression. So it's easy to make judgments about this, but this is a beautiful song written by someone who had a real command of language and who's describing things in beautiful images. He's an artist."

"The psychiatrist Mark Epstein," I said, "wrote a book with the title *Going to Pieces without Falling Apart.*"

"And that's the same thing as practicing how to feel sad without being sad. If you don't fall apart, there's something wrong with you [*laughing*]. We're all going to fall apart, we all experience that. All of us fall into pieces eventually, but sometimes you have that experience ahead of time, and then you can later say, Do I want to stay in all these pieces? Or am I going to do a little sweeping and try to fix things up a bit."

"Let's talk about 'Penny Lane,'" I suggested to Laurie, "because like 'Strawberry Fields Forever' it's also a kind of painting. But 'Penny Lane' is filled with light and blue suburban skies and what William Wordsworth called 'the everyday sublime,' and it seems to exemplify the answer that the Chinese Buddhist master Nanquan gave when asked 'What is the Way?,' and he responded, 'Ordinary Mind is the Way.'"

"It certainly does," Laurie said. "'Penny Lane' is daily life observed through a transparent lens. In a way this song reminds me of Suzanne Vega's 'Tom's Diner'—very simple observations of people who are living their lives. But in 'Penny Lane' it's not 'I see a man walking.' No, it's I see a banker, I see a fireman, I see a barber, it's people with specific jobs who are doing the kind of role-playing you have to do in life. Everyone's playing the role that's expected of them.

"What's really lovely about this is its seeming normality. The song's not criticizing these people for doing the jobs that they do. It's just a very colorful picture of them, and when you see them it's up to you to say, 'Who are these people really?' That's the thing you're asking but Paul's just saying: here they are doing their jobs. Cutting hair. Cleaning the fire engine. These are hyperreal pictures with a lot of detail in them, not like 'Strawberry Fields,' which is very abstract. 'Penny Lane' has stuff in it— a portrait of the queen, photographs of people's haircuts, a motorcar, poppies in a tray. . . . By the way, what does 'four of fish and finger pies' mean?"

"Do you really want to know?"

"Sure."

"Well, okay, you asked. 'Four of fish' meant the fourpence price of a packet of fish and chips, and 'finger pies' refers to the fingering that boys would do to girls when they were waiting for the bus in the shelter of the roundabout. As Paul once explained, 'It was a nice little joke for the Liverpool lads who like a bit of smut.' . . . Well, you asked!"

"Thanks for that!" Laurie said, laughing. "It's good to know that there's a bit of smut in the song because everything else seems squeaky clean here."

"Don't be so sure," I told her. "I read a sly and uproarious article online in which the writer Alex Markham asserts that the entire song is filled with double entendres and sexual innuendos. Regarding the banker wearing his mac—well, the writer informs us that in Liverpool the word *mac* was a slang word for condom."

"Really?"

"And then he says that the fireman who carries a portrait of the queen in his pocket is . . . well, I'll leave that image to your imagination."

"He likes to keep his fire engine clean," Laurie observed, "he's got a thing for cleanliness, he's a little fussy. He takes the queen into every fire. Everyone is playing a role in this song."

"The nurse is certainly playing a role," I said, "and she knows she's in a play."

"And in this play," Laurie continued, "there's a man who's playing a barber, a man who's playing a banker, and a man who's playing a fireman. Paul's drawing hyperreal, supercolorful portraits, and you see this Penny Lane neighborhood clearly. It's very prosaic, everyone's doing their jobs, they stop and say hello—'hey, how's it going?'—but then you begin to notice that some of them are a little bit quirky: the barber's showing photos of every head he's had the pleasure to know, the fireman's in love with the queen, the banker never wears a mac."

"I think the interpreter of this song may be playing us!" I said.

"Yes, it's very tongue in cheek, but it's lovely that way. It's lighthearted, which I like very much. To me the whole song is a painting by David Hockney. Superbright, blue suburban skies, and everyone has a certain clichéd simplicity to them. Paul sings 'There beneath the blue suburban skies I sit,' and it's as if he's just sitting watching this movie—it's a movie, it's a play—where people are role-playing, but there's a fair degree of freedom within that. They're not doing drudgery jobs, they're really individuals. And then there's the pretty nurse who's selling poppies from a tray—she's the only female in the song—and suddenly everything comes into focus. But why is she selling poppies?"

"Because it's Remembrance Day," I explained, "which takes place every November 11 in Great Britain. People buy artificial poppies in order to pay tribute to the soldiers who died in the trenches during World War I, but also to fallen soldiers in other wars as well."

"But why poppies?"

"Because of the poppies that grew among the soldiers' grave sites in the fields of Flanders."

"So the nurse is telling you to remember all the dead. And here they are. Remember these people, they're poppies."

"You mean the soldiers who have died?"

"Yes, but also *all* the people in this song."

"As if these people were already dead or are going to be dead?"

"Yeah, she's in a play, she feels like she's in a play. *This whole thing is a play,* and she's the play's star who's saying, Remember these people. And I think that the person who's sitting watching this play is also watching her, he's looking at all the characters he's conjured up out of nothing and he wants them all to come together for a moment, but he doesn't include the nurse because she's still remembering these guys—it's a guy's song— and then at the end of the song they meet up at the barbershop. You see the barber shaving a customer, the banker's waiting for a trim, and then the fireman rushes in from the pouring rain. So there are five people in this play: the banker, the barber, the fireman, the viewer who's singing the song, and the one who remembers. And that makes for a very full play, and it's very strange, very strange."

"It's interesting," I pointed out, "that although 'Penny Lane' takes place beneath a blue suburban sky, all of a sudden the fireman rushes in from the pouring rain."

"It rains twice in this song," Laurie observed. "It's pouring outside, so I guess the fireman's free to get a haircut because he knows that if there's a fire, it's going to be put out by the rain [*laughing*]. So he'll take this moment to rush in and get a quick trim, and he's got that portrait of the queen in his pocket, and as we know he takes the queen into every fire, and he's also got an hourglass. This guy is really eccentric. All of these people are really out there!"

"But you've previously described all of these characters as being so normal," I reminded her.

"Well, they've got jobs, but I think that Paul's just saying that the *normal* is very strange. That's what this is about. It's a play that we don't know we're in, but we are anyway."

"As Alice says in *Alice's Adventures in Wonderland,* 'Curiouser and curiouser.'"

"Right. Curiouser and curiouser. It's very Alice in Wonderland. 'I'm late! I'm late! For a very important date!' says the White Rabbit. 'No time to say "hello, goodbye," I'm late! I'm late!'

And maybe the rabbit is carrying an hourglass. You're in a dream-world here because it's all 'meanwhile back.' Penny Lane isn't *out there,* it's back inside his head, it's in his ears and in his eyes—he says that four times. This isn't a real place, it's all about the memory of Penny Lane, it's Penny Lane remembered."

"The artist Jack Yeats remarked: 'No one creates . . . the artist assembles memories.'"

"That's a really good way to put it."

"And Gaston Bachelard wrote: 'The seasons of memory are eternal because they are faithful to the colors of the first time. In our reverie we see our illustrated universe once more with its childhood colors.'"

"Bingo!" Laurie exclaimed. "Those hot childhood colors! And your mind is new, which is a bracing thought."

"That reminds me," I said, "of the poet William Carlos Williams's great statement: 'A new world is just a new mind.'"

"That's exactly the point. You put all the teachings aside and make your mind new. Never use old formulas to put on top of some new situation. Just look and see things with your beginner's mind. And how many of us can do that? When you shock yourself or when someone shocks you by presenting you with a new image, it's like, wow, I never saw it like that before, but I know what you mean. *That* is beginner's mind. Start there. In fact *end* there. It's kind of the same."

"When Bachelard talks about 'seeing our illustrated universe once more with its childhood colors,'" I said, "it makes me think that 'Penny Lane' could be turned into a beautiful full-color children's picture book."

"And one that is full of light and air," Laurie agreed. "It's completely visual—it's a play, it's a movie, it's a children's picture book—and you can stroll through Penny Lane, whereas 'Strawberry Fields' is claustrophobic, you're hemmed in, but here the sky is open."

"The color of 'Penny Lane' is blue," I said, "and the color of 'Strawberry Fields Forever' is red. When I interviewed John Lennon in 1968, he told me, 'Strawberry Field was a place near where I lived in Liverpool that happened to be a Salvation Army home. But Strawberry Fields—I mean, I have visions of *strawberry fields!*'

"When we began our conversation today, you told me that you envisioned Strawberry Fields as your magic childhood dream island in Lake Ellyn. When I envision Strawberry Fields I have visions of an enormous field of dazzling red opium poppies, so I think I may have imported the pretty nurse's poppies into my own dream vision and crossbred them with the strawberries of Strawberry Fields. And I may have also been subconsciously recalling the field of intoxicating red poppies that Dorothy falls asleep in, overcome by their fumes, just when she was about to enter the Emerald City in *The Wonderful Wizard of Oz*. It's a field that the Wicked Witch of the West—who's perhaps the Greek god Morpheus in disguise—has conjured up in an attempt to block her from entering the city."

"Like my dream island," Laurie told me, "your field of poppies is a dreamspace, and it's a beautiful one. And Morpheus is part of it. [Morpheus was the Greek god of dreams and the son of Hypnos, the god of sleep.] To me, it's the strawberry part of that wonderful Zen Buddhist tale about a man who's being chased by a tiger, and he falls over a cliff, and he's desperately trying to hold on to a vine, and the tiger's just a few feet above him, and down below are two other tigers. And as he looks up, he sees a little strawberry just above his head, and he knows that if he lets go of that vine he's going to fall down, and then two mice come out of the bushes and start gnawing on the vine. But the strawberry looks so delicious, and as he reaches up and tries to pick the strawberry he's thinking, *Let's go for it . . .*"

"And what happens?"

"Well, he falls, but the story doesn't tell you that. I think that it's a story about letting go. I mean, why would the man want to reach for that strawberry and lose his life like that? But in fact, we're losing our lives all the time when we reach for things. The strawberry is temptation and beauty and lusciousness and childhood and fullness, and the poppy is the temptation of death and sleep, and as I mentioned earlier the ultimate dream state is death. But let's also remember that strawberries and poppies both have that bright red blood of life in them.

"To me, 'Penny Lane' and 'Strawberry Fields Forever' are both dreams, and they're both about the fact that we're asleep. 'Penny Lane' is a dream in which people are in a play and they can't get out of it, they're trapped in their roles, and it's the very deep sleep of people who don't realize that they're doing that. They're like sleepwalkers going through the motions, but they're very vividly painted. And 'Strawberry Fields' is a lucid dream, and it's one that goes on forever. Both of them are complicated dreams, but 'Strawberry Fields' is in soft focus and 'Penny Lane' is in sharp focus. One's a strawberry, one's a poppy, but it's the same dream, it's the same wondering: What is real? Is a strawberry more real than a poppy? [*Laughing*] I don't know, but both songs ask the same question: What's real? Is there a more important question than that?"

"Perhaps only 'To be or not to be,'" I suggested. "And speaking of that question, it once came to me in a flash that what Hamlet really should have said was 'To be *and* not to be. *That* is the answer.' What do you think?"

"I like it," said Laurie, laughing. "You should write a play about that. But maybe this book you're writing *is* your play about that."

"I may think I'm writing a play, but I'm in it anyway! And so are you, right?"

"Yes," Laurie replied, "we're both in this play together."

ACKNOWLEDGMENTS

Go—not knowing where; bring—not knowing what; the path is long,
the way unknown; the hero knows not how to arrive there by himself.
  —**Russian proverb**

I am inestimably grateful to the five guiding spirits and companions on my journey—Laurie Anderson, Bill Frisell, Richard Gere, Margaret Klenck, and Jonathan F. P. Rose—who led the way and who took me down to Strawberry Fields and then back to Penny Lane and in whose footsteps it was a joy and honor to follow.

Immeasurable thanks to Erik Anderson, an editor "way beyond compare."

Also at the University of Minnesota Press I am especially indebted to its director, Douglas Armato; the managing editor, Laura Westlund; the production manager, Daniel Ochsner; and to Shelby Connelly, Eliza Edwards, Emily Hamilton, Carina Bolaños Lewen, Emma Saks, Maggie Sattler, Heather Skinner, and Matt Smiley. Great thanks to my incomparable copy editor, Paula Dragosh; to the book's proofreader, Anna Lux; and special thanks to the jacket designer, Victor Mingovits.

For their abiding help and encouragement I give heartfelt thanks to Doris del Castillo, Lili Chopra, Calle Dieker, Annie Druyan, Ernie Eban, Laura García Lorca, Elizabeth Garnsey, Philippe Goldin, Jonas Herbsman,

Joanne Howard, Alice Michel, Joséphine Michel, Stephen Nachmano-
vitch, Lucia della Paolera, Uma Thurman, and Anne Waldman.

I am deeply grateful to my literary agents, Michael V. Carlisle and
Michael Mungiello, at InkWell Management.

✛

It is estimated that more than two thousand books have been written
about the Beatles. Among them, the following have been invaluable for
my own book.

> *The Beatles Anthology,* by the Beatles, published in 2000 as
>   part of the Beatles' Anthology film project. It presents the
>   Beatles' life recollections in their own words, as well as
>   those of (among others) George Martin, Neil Aspinall,
>   and Derek Taylor.
> *Beatles '66: The Revolutionary Year,* by Steve Turner
> *Paul McCartney: Many Years from Now,* by Barry Miles
> *The Beatles Recording Sessions,* by Mark Lewisohn
> *All You Need Is Ears,* by George Martin
> *Here, There, and Everywhere,* by Geoff Emerick and Howard
>   Massey
> *John Lennon,* by Philip Norman
> *Lennon: The Man, the Myth, the Music,* by Tim Riley
> *The Beatles: The Authorised Biography,* by Hunter Davies
> *Revolution in the Head: The Beatles' Records and the Sixties,*
>   by Ian MacDonald

I am also indebted to the hundreds of newspaper and magazine articles,
interviews, blogs, scholarly papers, videos, and essays about the Beatles,
Liverpool, and "Penny Lane" and "Strawberry Fields Forever," all of which
were indispensable resources. I especially want to call attention to and

praise two of those essays, "The Power of Two," by Joshua Wolf Shenk, which was published in *The Atlantic* in 2014 and was adapted from his book *Powers of Two: Finding the Essence of Innovation in Creative Pairs,* and an essay by Adam Gopnik that is the most insightful piece of writing I have read about those two songs, which was published in the book *In Their Lives: Great Writers on Great Beatles Songs,* edited by Andrew Blauner.

JONATHAN COTT is the author and editor of more than forty books. He has written for *Rolling Stone,* the *New York Times, The New Yorker,* and the *Washington Post.* He is author of *Days That I'll Remember: Spending Time with John Lennon and Yoko Ono* and coauthor of the text for *The Beatles Get Back,* a book included in the original 1969 box set of the *Let It Be* album. He interviewed Paul McCartney for *Rolling Stone* in 2009 on the fiftieth anniversary of Buddy Holly's death, and he completed a nine-hour interview with John Lennon three days before Lennon's death that was originally published in *Rolling Stone* and later reprinted in his book *Listening: Interviews, 1970–1989* (Minnesota, 2020). He is also the author of *Pipers at the Gates of Dawn: The Wisdom of Children's Literature* (Minnesota, 2020).